THE
RACING POST
QUIZ
BOOK
1,000 questions on horseracing

DEDICATION

This book is dedicated to my son Dan who has been bombarded with questions during the entirety of this project and even, when pressed, deigned to answer the odd one!

Published in 2019 by Racing Post

27 Kingfisher Court, Hambridge Road, Newbury, Berkshire, RG14 5SJ

Copyright © Mart Matthews 2019

The right of Mart Matthews to be identified as the author of this work has been asserted by him in accordance with the Copyright, Designs and Patents Act 1988.

10 9 8 7 6 5 4 3 2 1

A catalogue record for this book is available from the British Library.

Please note: All questions and answers are valid up to mid-June 2019. The outcome of some races between that date and publication may affect the odd question.

ISBN 978-1-83950-014-5

Cover design by Samantha Creedon

Typeset by Fiona Pike

Printed in the UK by CPI Books, Croydon

THE
RACING POST
QUIZ
BOOK

1,000 questions on horseracing

Mart Matthews

ACKNOWLEDGEMENTS

Heartfelt thanks are due to my old friend Dave Ashforth for his excellent technical assistance on a damn clever little device I'm led to believe is known as a computer.

Thanks also go to Ian Carnaby for his hospitality at Brighton racecourse over more years than I care to remember and for providing an initial format for my quizzes.

Thanks too to Liz Ampairee, Brough Scott and Jimmy Pugh at Racing Post Books for giving me the opportunity in the first place.

ABOUT THE QUIZ COMPILER

Mart Matthews has been a milkman, a betting shop manager, college lecturer and 'progress chaser' in an aircraft factory. Whatever he was supposed to be chasing he clearly never caught up with it!

Now he spends his days knocking out quizzes like the one you are currently looking at. His only concern is that, at the age of 72, he may have peaked too soon!

IF

(with apologies to Kipling and his cakes!)

If you've ever read the Racing Post
With your breakfast eggs on toast

If you've ever had a score
On a ride of Ryan Moore

If you've ever used the Hills
To try to pay off all your bills

If you've ever borrowed from a parson
To get a bet on Willie Carson

If you've ever been a loser
Then put it right with S. De Sousa

If you've ever had a great night out
Courtesy of Sir Michael Stoute

If you've ever done holiday planning
Based on winnings from Joe Fanning

If you've ever found Jamie Spencer
To be a useful cash dispenser

If you've lost your chips on Donald McCain
Or ever prayed for overnight rain

If you've read Fifty Shades of Hay
But still can't make your racing pay

Then you might like to solve a little tester
About the deeds of a man called Lester

But that is just the one example
Of a thousand you could sample

If you can tell a Hatfield from a McCoy
This book should bring you hours of joy

In this, the latest quiz on racing
We cover the Flat as well as chasing

So get stuck into your copy now, don't steal mine,
You can't go wrong at twelve ninety-nine!

FOREWORD

Whether a novice, Group-class performer or just a grizzled old handicapper, this is a book that is guaranteed to give you many hours of pleasure and is extremely difficult to put down.

With 1,000 tantalising questions spread over 100 categories, the Racing Post Quiz Book has the capacity to fascinate and frustrate in equal measure.

As well as straightforward tests of memory there are also questions of a more cryptic nature, which require not just a bit of racing knowledge but also creative lateral thinking to answer them correctly.

From Terpsichorean Art to the Spanish Inquisition, from Tamla Motown to Sir Henry Cecil, the range of topics on which to display knowledge and ignorance is wide-ranging.

Pride at pulling an answer out of the fire contrasts sharply with knowing that an answer is on the edge of memory but frustratingly out of reach. Sadly for me these days, the latter outnumber the former!

Richard Hoiles, ITV Racing commentator

ACTORS, FILMS AND RELATED STUFF.

1. This very speedy 2013 winner of the Middle Park Stakes and Gimcrack Stakes for jockey Neil Callan and trainer Kevin Ryan was named after someone whose feet were almost as fast!

2. It was somewhat difficult to see this Saeed Bin Suroor-trained, Frankie Dettori-ridden winner of the Royal Hunt Cup at Ascot in 2010 but you might have been aware of the 1933 film adaptation of the H.G. Wells novel.

3. The Coventry Stakes and Gimcrack Stakes winner of 1962, whose connections were Geoffrey Brooke and Doug Smith, was possibly named after the larger than life character who John Wayne played in the film 'The Alamo.'

4. A very enterprising ride from Ryan Moore for Sir Michael Stoute saw them land the 2007 Eclipse Stakes at Sandown on a horse named for what Peter Sellers often said to Burt Kwouk in the Inspector Clouseau films.

5. He could have been a contender and he most certainly was one when he took the 2016 Ayr Gold Cup for jockey Tom Eaves and trainer Kevin Ryan!

6. Champagne Stakes success at Doncaster for Henry Cecil and Joe Mercer in 1980 with a horse named after a legendary British stage and screen actor.

7. This winner of the 2010 running of the Ayr Gold Cup for Frankie Dettori and Dandy Nicholls was an actor whose name will always be associated with Paul Newman.

8. Named for perhaps the most iconic film actor, this horse, trained by Richard Hannon and ridden by Sean Levey, had small wins at Doncaster and Lingfield before finishing fifth in Harzand's 2016 Derby. He is now trying obstacles with Nicky Henderson.

9. Noel Meade's winner of the 2002 Irish Grand National, ridden by Ross Geraghty, was surely named after Glenn Close's character in the movie "Fatal Attraction".

10. This stayer won the Irish St Leger in both the 1996 and 1997 runnings of the race. He was named after the main subject of the film, set in Nazi Germany, that came out in 1993, the role being played by Liam Neeson. At the Curragh the main roles were those of Stephen Craine and Kevin Prendergast.

QUIZ No 2

ADVERTISING.

"The large print giveth and the small print taketh away." Tom Waits.

1. In 1991 the sponsors of the Grand National must have thought they had died and gone to heaven when the horse named after their product actually won the race! What was it called?

2. Which camera manufacturer's catchphrase won the 1997 Doncaster Cup, trained by Henry Cecil and ridden by Kieren Fallon?

3. Which petroleum company's slogan was used to name the horse that won the 1965 running of the Portland Handicap at Doncaster? It was owned by Lord Derby, trained by Bernard van Cutsem and ridden by Doug Smith.

4. Those of us who grew up in the 1950s and 1960s could go to bed with Bournvita, Horlicks or the winner of the 1967 Ebor Handicap, trained by Bill Watts and ridden by Ernie Johnson. If we did we were assured of being 'happy girls and boys'.

5. The winner of the 1968 Triumph Hurdle, ridden by Jimmy Uttley and trained by Staff Ingham, was named after a box of matches made by Bryant and May and carrying a patriotic sentiment. What was it called?

6. Mr Fred Pontin, the owner of a well-known chain of holiday camps, changed the name of a horse called Gay Navarree to Pontin-Go on the grounds that it would be good for business. As the business expanded he called another horse Go-Pontinental. Between them, from 1964 to 1974, these two horses competed in the same race six times. Which race?

7. This might be the only horse named after a 600-year-old product that you inhale to help with a head cold. What a horse he was! Unbeaten in seven starts as a two-year-old, trained by the legendary John Porter, he won the 1888 Champion Stakes. Who was he?

8. If you still can't shift that cold try this remedy that won back-to-back Champion Hurdles in 1976 and 1977. That should do the trick!

9. In 1978, as a two-year-old, trained by Sir Michael Stoute and ridden by Greville Starkey, this horse won both Sandown's National Stakes and Ascot's Norfolk Stakes. It was named after a soft drinks company. Schhh... you know who!

10. Questions were asked by the powers that be about using products in the naming of horses when this one, alleged to give a meal 'man-appeal,' partnered by Michael Scudamore and trained by Willie Stephenson, won the 1959 Grand National.

'AFTER YOU SIR!'

All these horses share the prefix 'Sir.'

1. Which Sir did the business for Marcus Tregoning and Martin Dwyer in the 2006 Epsom Derby?

2. This Sir was successful in the 1979 Cesarewitch for Geoff Huffer and Mark Rimmer and since then the world of horseracing has got another one!

3. Trained by Ryan Price, this particular Sir gave Willie Carson an Ebor Handicap victory in 1976.

4. Which Sir, trained by Barry Hills, gave John Reid his sole Irish Derby success, in 1987?

5. This Sir, trained by Robert Alner and ridden by Andrew Thornton, ran three fine races when, firstly, he was second to Bindaree in the 2003 Welsh Grand National then, in the 2004 Cheltenham Gold Cup, he was second to Best Mate and, finally, in 2005, in the same race, he was third to Kicking King. Who was he?

6. Lester Piggott described this Raymond Guest-owned, Vincent O'Brien-trained winner of the 1968 Derby as the best horse he had ever sat on. What was his name?

7. Which Sir won the 2007 Gimcrack Stakes at York for Jamie Spencer and James Fanshawe?

8. The Derby was named in honour of the 12th Earl of Derby but he only managed to win the race once, in 1787. His winner was named after a character in Sheridan's play 'The School for Scandal'. What was he called?

9. Not many horses have won the French 2,000 Guineas and followed it up the next season by winning the Lincoln Handicap. This one did, in 1924.

10. In April 2000, Walter Swinburn rode the final winner of his career as a top jockey when this horse, possibly named after an English maritime hero of the late 16th century, went past the post first at Brighton.

'ANIMAL HOUSE.'

All these horses' names contain those of animals.

1. He may be small but he hounded the opposition enough to land the stayers' double of Ascot Gold Cup and Goodwood Cup for Dick Hern and Willie Carson in 1983.

2. What a year this grey colt had in 2018, finishing the season with victory in Ascot's Queen Elizabeth II Stakes after taking the Dante, Eclipse, Juddmonte International and Irish Champion Stakes for John Gosden and Oisin Murphy.

3. It sounds as if this beast escaped from the Vatican to win the King Edward VII Stakes for trainer Sir Michael Stoute at Royal Ascot in 2006.

4. This horse achieved a magnificent Grand National double in 2018 and 2019 for jockey Davy Russell and trainer Gordon Elliott, a feat last achieved in 1974.

5. Winner of Ascot's Queen Alexandra Stakes for Joe Fanning and Mark Johnston in 2015 and again in 2017.

6. After finishing second in the 2007 Epsom Oaks this rapidly improving filly won four consecutive Group 1 races for trainer Aidan O'Brien.

7. A much-loved stayer owned and bred by Michael Owen, trained by Tom Dascombe and usually ridden by Richard Kingscote. He won, among other races, the 2013 Goodwood Cup and 2014 Irish St Leger.

8. This small grey had a big heart and won the Grand Nationals of 1868 and 1871. If the rock group Genesis had their way and he did lie down on Broadway he would stop the traffic!

9. Royal Ascot's Norfolk Stakes went the way of this reptile for trainer Peter Chapple-Hyam and jockey John Reid in 1993.

10. This winner of the 1930 Cheveley Park Stakes may have stepped out of a Visconti film but certainly can't change her spots!

THE ARC.

1. Ninth of 11 in the legendary clash between Grundy and Bustino, this horse won the 1975 Arc.

2. Why was the well-known saying 'two heads are better than one' appropriate in Ivanjica's 1976 Arc?

3. 1997 was the last year in which the name of the winning horse and jockey started with the same letter. Who was involved?

4. Since 1920, when the Arc was first run, only one horse beginning with a 'Z' has won it; pretty impressively as well. Who was it?

5. Which jockey has won the Arc the most times?

6. Which horse won the race in 1984 and was denied doing it again the following year by the stewards, who awarded the race to Pat Eddery on Rainbow Quest?

7. 2003 was the last year in which the current French Derby winner won the Arc. It was ridden by Christophe Soumillon and trained by Alain de Royer-Dupre. What was it called?

8. The Arc's regular venue, Longchamp, was not available for the 2016 and 2017 runnings of the race. Where was it held instead?

9. Who was the last filly to win the French Oaks and Arc in the same season?

10. Which father and son, both jockeys, have won the Arc five times between them?

QUIZ No 6

'ASCOT ATTACK' – PART ONE – FOREIGN RIDERS AT ROYAL ASCOT.

1. Who was the American jockey who won the King's Stand Stakes in successive years, firstly in 1986 on Last Tycoon for trainer Robert Collet; then with Bluebird for Vincent O'Brien?

2. Which American jockey, riding for the Queen and Sir Michael Stoute, won the Duke of Edinburgh Stakes (formerly the Bessborough Stakes) on Blueprint in 1999?

3. Which Australian jockey rode Gildoran in the 1985 Ascot Gold Cup when he won the race for a second time for trainer Barry Hills?

4. Who rode Scenic Blast when it won the King's Stand Stakes in 2009?

5. Who was aboard Lady Aurelia when she won the King's Stand Stakes in 2017?

6. Who won the Norfolk Stakes for trainer Wesley Ward in both 2013 with No Nay Never and in 2018 with Shang Shang Shang?

7. Which Hong Kong-based Australian jockey won the King's Stand Stakes with Little Bridge in 2012?

8. Who partnered Black Caviar to victory in the 2012 Diamond Jubilee Stakes?

9. Who rode Miss Andretti at Royal Ascot when she won the King's Stand Stakes in 2007? The jockey's got the answer!

10. Who was Takeover Target's jockey when it won the King's Stand in 2006?

'ASCOT ATTACK' – PART TWO – THE RECENT TREND OF OVERSEAS-TRAINED WINNERS.

1. Which French-based trainer won the King's Stand Stakes with the Christophe Lemaire-ridden Chineur in 2005?

2. Undrafted, ridden by Frankie Dettori, took the Diamond Jubilee Stakes for which American trainer in 2015?

3. Which Aussie trainer was successful in winning the King's Stand Stakes in 2009 with Scenic Blast?

4. Which Hong Kong-based trainer's Little Bridge won the 2012 King's Stand Stakes?

5. The overseas plundering of Ascot's top prizes is relatively recent but in 1956 an undefeated Italian-trained colt called Ribot thrilled the King George crowd when ridden by Enrico Camici. Who trained Ribot?

6. Which Australian was responsible for training the brilliant Black Caviar, winner of the 2012 Diamond Jubilee Stakes at Royal Ascot?

7. Which Chantilly-based trainer sent Nuclear Debate and Gerard Mosse over to Ascot to pick up the King's Stand Stakes in 2000?

8. Which Australian trainer saddled Miss Andretti when the speedster won the 2007 running of the King's Stand Stakes?

9. Which Aussie performed the feat of training Choisir to win twice at Royal Ascot in 2003, taking both the Golden Jubilee and King's Stand Stakes?

10. Why don't we end with another Aussie! Which trainer won the King's Stand Stakes in 2006 with the aptly named Takeover Target?

QUIZ No 8

ASSORTED COLOURS.

All these horses have a colour in their names. Can you identify them?

1. This 1966 Triumph Hurdle winner is not something you want to encounter when out driving in winter!

2. James Doyle and Michael Bell grab Ascot's Gold Cup in 2017.

3. Emotional 4,000th winner for Pat Eddery in the 1997 running of the St Leger.

4. In the 1970s Jim Dreaper claimed three Irish Grand Nationals with this horse.

5. A nation is always relieved to get this under its belt at an Olympics and on Boxing Day at Kempton Park in 2000 the Doumen family were doubtless happy when this horse got the job done.

6. The Gimcrack victor of 1969, owned by David Robinson, trained by Paul Davey and ridden by Frankie Durr.

7. An Irish Derby winner for Dermot Weld and Pat Smullen in 2004.

8. A colt trained by Sir Michael Stoute who sounds like a contradiction in terms. He had a great year in 1986 when, after being runner-up to Dancing Brave in the 2,000 Guineas, he went on to land the July Cup and Haydock Sprint Cup.

9. In 1967 this precious stone dead-heated with Pia, that year's Oaks winner, in Doncaster's Park Hill Stakes. The horse's connections were George Moore and Noel Murless.

10. You are supposed to slow down when this colour appears but this French speedball had no intention of letting Yves Saint-Martin pull up when winning the 1970 running of Ascot's King's Stand Stakes.

AUSTRALIAN JOCKEYS – ONE FOR THE OLDIES!

Back in the 1950s and 1960s British racing hosted a significant number of Flat jockeys from 'Down Under'. This is by way of a tribute to them, with apologies to those who didn't make the ten.

1. The pioneer of Australian riders, between 1934 and 1956 he won 12 Classics, including the Derby on three occasions with My Love, Galcador and Lavandin. Who was he?

2. This Aussie jockey rode horses in Britain for Vincent O'Brien, most notably when landing the Oaks in 1965 on Long Look.

3. This jockey must have thought he was the luckiest alive when he got the ride on number 22 in the 1965 Derby. He became part of a legend that got even bigger at Longchamp in the Arc.

4. Among this Aussie's many wins in the 1960s were both Guineas and the St Leger while in the 1970s he secured the Ascot Gold Cup for John Dunlop on Ragstone and was on board when Sheikh Mohammed won his first race as an owner in Britain in 1977 with Hatta, also trained by John Dunlop.

5. A broken leg sustained at Newbury in 1969 ended this Aussie's career, but not before he had won the Nunthorpe for Pat Rohan on Althrey Don in 1964. Who was he?

6. This jockey from 'Down Under' had an excellent 1964, landing both the 2,000 Guineas on Baldric II and Ascot's King George aboard Nasram II. He won the latter race again in 1973 on the brilliant Dahlia.

7. This rider won the 1962 Derby for trainer Vincent O'Brien on Larkspur but sadly was killed in a race in France later that year.

8. This Australian won three British Classics, all for trainer Paddy Prendergast. They were the 1963 Oaks on Noblesse, the same year's St Leger on Ragusa and the following year's 1,000 Guineas on Pourparler.

9. Champion jockey on four occasions, winner of four Classics, including the 1964 Derby on Santa Claus and the 1966 Derby on Charlottown, he was probably the most popular of the Aussie jockeys and stayed on in Britain as a trainer when his riding days were over.

10. My personal favourite, he twice won the 1,000 Guineas in the 1960s on Abermaid and Night Off but his finest moments came with back-to-back Arcs in 1968 and 1969 on Vaguely Noble and Levmoss, on whom he also won the Ascot Gold Cup.

QUIZ No 10

BIRDS.

The following horses all have a bird in their name.

1. This species of seabird was a very smart filly who, as a three-year-old, won the 1983 Champion Stakes under Steve Cauthen for trainer Barry Hills. The next year she signed off her racing career by taking the Benson & Hedges Gold Cup at York for the same connections.

2. Ridden on both occasions by Lester Piggott, this top two-year-old colt won both the Prix Robert Papin and the Prix Morny in 1970 but was extremely unlucky to have been foaled in the same year as Brigadier Gerard and Mill Reef, both of whom he followed home in the 1971 2,000 Guineas.

3. This nocturnal bird, trained by Peter Easterby, ran out the winner of the Cheltenham Gold Cup in 1981 for an amateur jockey. That was one Mr Jim Wilson who had been 'gifted' the horse.

4. Equally brilliant on the Flat and over hurdles, this much-loved son of Sea-Bird was versatility personified as, between 1977 and 1981, he collected two Chester Cups, the Ebor Handicap and two Champion Hurdles for trainer Peter Easterby.

5. This bird of prey, trained by Geoff Barling and ridden by Pat Eddery, won the Ascot Gold Cup of 1972 in the stewards' room. A few weeks later he won the Goodwood Cup without needing such assistance.

6. Ridden by Mark Dwyer and trained by Richard Price, this peaceful sort appears to have been falling apart in the 1994 Champion Hurdle but still won the race!

7. It wasn't a shock that a certain Irish trainer won the 2017 Derby but the horse he won it with certainly was. Allowed to start at 40-1 he flew past everything close home up the middle of the track.

8. Arguably the greatest horse to grace the Flat, it never seemed like a contest until Frankel's arrival on the scene. This colt won the 1965 Derby and Arc with disdainful ease.

9. I expect members of his family gathered in nearby trees and made a lot of noise when this horse came over from France to win the 1976 St Leger, with Yves Saint-Martin doing the steering.

10. Trained by Aidan O'Brien this colt was not short of ability; far from it. However, his achievements were sketchy. Runner-up in both the 2,000 Guineas and the Derby in 2002, beaten by stablemates on each occasion, his finest hour came in the following year's Lockinge Stakes at Newbury, where it is hard to find enough superlatives to describe his performance.

'THE BLUES.'

All these winners have the prefix 'Blue.'

1. This horse, ridden by Eddie Ahern and trained by Jeremy Noseda, bombed up Ascot's straight to take the 2004 Norfolk Stakes.

2. The only twentieth century Oaks winner with 'Blue' in its name, trained by Dermot Weld and ridden by Lester Piggott. She won the 1981 renewal.

3. Ridden by Ernie Johnson, this horse's success in the 1973 Ayr Gold Cup was an early indication of Sir Michael Stoute's ability as a trainer.

4. Which horse, later the title of a BBC TV children's programme, was the last peacetime winner of the Derby before World War II? It was jockey Eph Smith's solitary Derby success.

5. Named after some people's idea of the worst day of the week, this Steve Drowne-ridden and Roger Charlton-trained charge landed the 2005 Cambridgeshire Handicap plus the Zetland Gold Cup for good measure.

6. David Loder and Mick Kinane cleaned up with this winner of the Queen Mary Stakes and Cheveley Park Stakes in 1995.

7. Both William Buick and James Doyle have won Ascot's King's Stand Stakes on this colt. Who is he?

8. Perhaps Frankie Dettori put some of this up after winning the 1,000 Guineas of 2011 for Godolphin!

9. Multi-purpose horse who took the Swinton Hurdle at Haydock for Graham Lee and Andy Turnell in 2008 before turning to the Flat to land Sandown's Henry II Stakes in 2011 for Daniel Tudhope and David O'Meara.

10. Winner of Ascot's New Stakes (later renamed the Norfolk Stakes) in 1952, the horse's name reflects a 1950 film that led to the BBC TV series Dixon of Dock Green.

QUIZ No 12

BOOKMAKERS.

1. A company that shares its name with a football club was founded in 1924 and is now based in Malta. Which company is it?

2. Complete the unlikely slogan – "Never a Quarrel __ __ __"

3. Which bookmaker from Essex is widely associated with the word 'Bismarck'?

4. Cyril Stein was chairman of which firm from 1966 to 1993?

5. Which bookmaker, after inheriting his father's company, was the first to move his business off-shore for tax purposes when he set up in Gibraltar in 1998?

6. Which colourful figure on the racecourse in the 1960s and 1970s owned a chain of betting shops in Glasgow and a yellow Rolls-Royce before falling foul of the authorities in 1978?

7. One of the shrewdest and most fearless of bookmakers, this man started making a book in 1934 and although the company he founded has had its ups and downs, it still controls around 25 per cent of the UK market. Who was he?

8. Which bookmaker is associated with Stoke City Football Club and a sometimes disembodied Ray Winstone?

9. Which likeable course bookmaker lost close on £1 million at Ascot in September 1996, courtesy of Frankie Dettori's 'Magnificent Seven'? He had only ended up there because of a traffic jam!

10. Which course bookmaker was known for regularly fielding some hefty wagers from JP McManus at the Cheltenham Festival?

THE CHELTENHAM FESTIVAL.

1. Which four horses are commemorated in statues at Cheltenham racecourse?

2. Up to 2019, who is the only owner to have won the Cheltenham Gold Cup in three successive decades?

3. Which horse was never out of the frame in the Queen Mother Champion Chase in the four years from 1994 to 1997?

4. A familiar surname was attached to the winning jockey in the 2019 Champion Hurdle, but the first name had changed. Who were the successful horse and jockey?

5. Who was the only horse to be in the frame in two of Best Mate's three Gold Cup wins?

6. In 2001, the Gold Cup did not take place due to an outbreak of foot and mouth disease. A replacement race was later run at Sandown. The winner doubled as a town in Wiltshire. What was the horse called?

7. Willie Mullins had to wait a while to get his hands on the Cheltenham Gold Cup but it finally arrived in 2019 courtesy of which horse?

8. Which horse, within an ace of being put down early in his life, trained by Jane Pilkington and ridden by amateur jockey Mr Jim Wilson, won Cheltenham's Coral Golden Hurdle (later the Pertemps Hurdle) in 1979, 1980 and 1981, when he was 13 years old? The next winner of the race was called Tall Order, which was an apt comment on the achievement.

9. Which Fulke Walwyn-trained horse finished third, third again, first and then second in the Gold Cup from 1971 to 1974?

10. Which horse became the first novice in over 40 years to win the Gold Cup when, in 2015, he provided both jockey Nico de Boinville and trainer Mark Bradstock with their first wins in the race?

CITIES.

1. Ancient city wins 1979 Derby for Dick Hern and Willie Carson.

2. American city and TV series trained by Luca Cumani and ridden by Ray Cochrane took the 1986 Cambridgeshire Handicap at Newmarket.

3. Towering success for this city in the 1806 Derby!

4. City known for Tamla-Motown, she won the 1980 running of the Prix de l'Arc de Triomphe under Pat Eddery.

5. Precocious two-year-old who carried all before him in 2001, culminating in a win in the Breeders' Cup Juvenile for Mick Kinane and Aidan O'Brien.

6. French city that won the 1991 St Leger for Khalid Abdullah, Andre Fabre and Pat Eddery.

7. Home to Frasier Crane and Jimi Hendrix, this city lent its name to a phenomenal American racehorse that won the coveted Triple Crown in 1977. Who was he?

8. Ascot's Victoria Cup winner in 1968 must have made connections eternally grateful!

9. Indian city that triumphed in the 2000 Chester Cup for jockey Gary Bardwell and trainer Amanda Perrett.

10. This Eastern European city, often riven by conflict, won the 1996 Irish Derby for jockey Pat Shanahan and trainer Dermot Weld.

CLASSICAL COMPOSERS.

1. Mick Kinane and Aidan O'Brien teamed up to win Royal Ascot's 2007 Queen's Vase with this horse, named after the composer whose Adagietto from his Fifth Symphony was used in the film 'Death in Venice.'

2. This horse was given a name it was always going to be impossible to live up to – and it didn't – except once, in the 2009 Dewhurst Stakes when, under Ryan Moore, it stormed up at 33-1.

3. This horse showed an awesome turn of foot under Mick Kinane to land the 1999 July Cup at Newmarket. It was named after a composer whose 'Rite of Spring' caused people to sit up and take notice by inciting a riot during its first performance!

4. According to the play and film concerning Mozart's life – 'Amadeus' – this jealous man was Mozart's mortal enemy but, assisted by Henry Cecil and Lester Piggott, he was successful in the 1983 Hungerford Stakes at Newbury.

5. A winner of Chester's Dee Stakes in 1975 for Barry Hills and Willie Carson, in the next decade he also provided the music for a celebrated performance by Torvill and Dean.

6. A truly great sprinter, this horse lived up to his name on a number of occasions for Mick Kinane and Aidan O'Brien, most notably in the 2001 July Cup at Newmarket.

7. This Coolmore-owned horse, named after a 19th century composer, produced a fitting Exacta for someone by finishing second to Khalid Abdullah's Distant Music in the 1999 Dewhurst Stakes at Newmarket.

8. In 2001, this horse, named after perhaps the daddy of all composers, finished third in three Group 1 races; the Eclipse Stakes, Irish Champion Stakes and Breeders' Cup Mile. Who was he?

9. Named after an Italian composer of the 16th and 17th centuries, in 1979 this Robert Sangster-owned and Vincent O'Brien-trained colt carried all before him as a two-year-old, being unbeaten in four races, including the Dewhurst Stakes with Lester Piggott on board, but never won again.

10. This horse, trained by John Gosden and named after a French composer, appropriately won the Prix Eugene Adam in 2009 before, in the following season, landing the big one – the Arlington Million.

CRYPTIC HORSES.

1. The winner of the Welsh Grand National in 1992 and the Scottish Grand National in 1993, trained by Martin Pipe and ridden by Mark Perrett, sounds like what an amateur athlete would do.

2. Fisherman's friend takes the 2003 Sussex Stakes at Goodwood for trainer Richard Hannon snr and jockey Pat Eddery.

3. This Frankie Dettori-ridden winner of the 2004 Prix de l'Abbaye was introduced in the Premier League in the 2019-20 season.

4. The winner of the 1937 Cesarewitch was a magazine, a drink and half of a seaside entertainment. What was it called?

5. A motorbike wins the 2002 Ascot Royal Hunt Cup for trainer Terry Mills and jockey Jimmy Fortune!

6. September 26, 2004 was the last day of the old Ascot before its reconstruction. The winner of the first race that day was a horse trained by Alan Jarvis and ridden by Kerrin McEvoy whose name is a Chelsea, Wimbledon and Millwall player's name backwards. What was the horse called?

7. Trainer James Bethell's winner of the Bunbury Cup in 2002, 2005 and 2006 becomes possessive and doesn't want to give the trophy back!

8. Why was it hard for the Nicky Henderson-trained, Eddie Ahern-ridden winner of the 2011 Ascot Stakes to see where she was going?

9. In 1964, Elvis Presley had one of these and spent three minutes trying to justify the relationship. The more up to date version won Ascot's Coronation Stakes in 1994, trained by Henry Cecil and ridden by Mick Kinane. What was it called?

10. When modern professional golfers fail to get a birdie on a par-five hole they often show their disappointment with the phrase that won the bet365 Gold Cup Chase at Sandown in 2015, trained by Paul Nicholls and ridden by Sean Bowen. What was it called?

CRYPTIC 1,000 GUINEAS.

You are given a clue and a year. Name the winning horses.

1. Fast group of ships. 1967.

2. Napoleon's nemesis. 1972.

3. Nighthawks enjoying themselves. 1975.

4. This one's got two numbers in its name. 1979.

5. Free drink! 1982.

6. There are a lot of these on Brighton beach. 1984.

7. For me, it's listening to Beethoven, for you it might be something else. 1989.

8. Opera composer dresses for bad weather. 1998.

9. Gallic entry for beauty contest. 2014.

10. Nippy season. 2017.

QUIZ No 18

CRYPTIC 2,000 GUINEAS.

You are given a clue and a year. Name the winning horses.

1. Scottish loch. 1983.

2. London thoroughfare on Monopoly board. 1958.

3. Conan Doyle character. 1971.

4. My son. 1973.

5. Palindromic winner. 1976.

6. United States President. 2006.

7. Steve Harley's rock group. 2007.

8. Probably didn't get much sleep under the circumstances! 2014.

9. Scottish golf course. 2015.

10. British Prime Minister. 2017.

CRYPTIC DERBY.

You are given a clue and a year. Name the winning horses.

1. Giant's Causeway had this attitude in spades. 1954.

2. Visits once a year. 1964.

3. Legendary exponent of Terpsichorean art. 1970.

4. Put out to sea. 1985.

5. Shipman or Crippen perhaps. 1992.

6. Eisenhower's role in World War Two. 1993.

7. Method of housing often more popular with the architect than the occupant. 1998.

8. Precedes giving evidence in court. 1999.

9. Imprisoned by the Inquisition in 1632 for being right! 2001.

10. Cowboy TV series. 2002.

QUIZ No 20

CRYPTIC OAKS.

You are given a clue and a year. Name the winning horses.

1. Early Simon and Garfunkel song. 1964.

2. You can have one of these in a business or a bed. 1969.

3. Scottish football club. 1977.

4. Famous choreographer. 1994.

5. Wordsworth contributed extensively to the sum of these. 1997.

6. Informally dressed. 2003.

7. Apparently very useful for contacting the dead. 2004.

8. Knock off work early. 2007.

9. We are told that a particular Saturday night TV show is full of this but I've never seen any evidence of it! 2013.

10. Terry McCann did a lot of this for Arthur Daley. 2016.

CRYPTIC ST LEGER.

You are given a clue and a year. Name the winning horses.

1. A sixth sense that something might be about to happen. 1953.

2. American State located between Illinois to the west and Ohio to the east. 1964.

3. Pleasant green area in south-west London. 2018.

4. Superstitious behaviour. 1982.

5. What you expect to be shortly after boarding a plane. 1946.

6. Short instrumental piece of music between sections of an orchestral work. 1969.

7. Bob Dylan was one. 2006.

8. Spiderman, Batman or the Lone Ranger, perhaps. 2011.

9. Pam Ayres wrote a lot of this. 2015.

10. Car or island. 2017.

QUIZ No 22

CRYPTIC GRAND NATIONAL.

You are given a clue and a year. Name the winning horses.

1. Comfortably off. 1972.

2. The garment business. 1976.

3. Towering Scottish landmark. 1980.

4. Greet a kid's comic. 1984.

5. Escaping butterfly. 2000.

6. Excellent wood for a logburner. 2007.

7. What Goldfinger said to James Bond in so many words. 2008.

8. Good advice if you're not in the best of health and your car breaks down! 2010.

9. Looks like rain again! 2015.

10. In the early 1960s Harry Secombe sang about wanting to do this. 2016.

CRYPTIC CHAMPION HURDLE.

You are given a clue and a year. Name the winning horses.

1. Not something Maradona could be accused of doing in 1986! 1963.

2. Shakespeare fouls up. 1975.

3. In 1836 the defenders of the Alamo decided to do this. 1997.

4. Religious meadow. 1978 and 1979.

5. Sounds as if he ran in a seller instead. 1982.

6. Words likely to be uttered by the proprietor of 'Open All Hours' after another error by his hapless assistant. 1993.

7. Perhaps he should have won the Northumberland Plate instead! 1996.

8. Chicken on vitamins. 2003.

9. Feline deposit. 2008.

10. Small insect caught in decidedly inclement weather. 2011 and 2013.

QUIZ No 24

CRYPTIC CHELTENHAM GOLD CUP.

You are given a clue and a year. Name the winning horses.

1. George, Andrew, David or Patrick for example. 1928.

2. A Marxist in the boat race, perhaps. 1945.

3. You sometimes need to do this to get someone to open the door! 1953.

4. Batsman reaches double figures. 1975.

5. Early jog. 1986.

6. Rodin masterpiece. 1987.

7. What an advert's supposed to help you do. 1999.

8. Stalingrad was one of these. 2006.

9. What I bought cost a shilling! 2013.

10. Lake District bigwig. 2014.

CRYPTIC QUEEN MOTHER CHAMPION CHASE.

You are given a clue and a year. Name the winning horses.

1. Name synonymous with heroic retreat of Allied troops during World War Two. 1965.

2. Arrowhead sailing through space. 1966.

3. Surname of Dennis Norden's writing partner. 1969.

4. Singular instance of product associated with Walkers, Smiths and Golden Wonder. 1971.

5. One more cloned sheep. 1980.

6. Building that only cost a dollar. 1986.

7. Wind blowing down a slope. 1991.

8. Russian aviator. 2003 and 2005.

9. If you came up against Wyatt Earp in a gunfight it would be useful to be good at this. 2015.

10. The piece of headgear the Pope wears on important occasions, I guess. 2017.

QUIZ No 26

CRYPTIC KING GEORGE VI CHASE.

You are given a clue and a year. Name the winning horses.

1. October 31st. 1952 and 1954.

2. A fruit, a duck, a language and a member of an elite group. 1957 and 1959.

3. Asleep. 1966.

4. In the early years of the 20th century, significantly south of here, this man left a tent uttering the words 'I may be some time'. 1969.

5. Where ex-footballer Joey keeps his money. 1993.

6. Singular Fellow. 1995 and 1996.

7. A dollar's worth of precious metal. 1980.

8. Monarch takes up football. 2004 and 2005.

9. Marathon. 2010 and 2012.

10. Actor's saviour. 2015.

CURRENT JOCKEYS – FLAT.

1. Which British jockey was responsible for Prince Bishop's success in the Dubai World Cup at Meydan in 2015 for trainer Saeed Bin Suroor?

2. Which up and coming jockey got Lightning Spear up to win the 2018 Sussex Stakes for trainer David Simcock?

3. Who rode Al Kazeem to victory in the 2013 Eclipse Stakes at Sandown for trainer Roger Charlton?

4. Which ex-jump jockey won the Northumberland Plate for trainer Jonjo O'Neill on Tominator in 2013?

5. Which jockey provided trainer David O'Meara with a Royal Ascot winner when taking the Wokingham Stakes aboard the eight-year-old Out Do in 2017?

6. Who became champion jockey for the first time in 2015?

7. Clive Cox's top sprinter Lethal Force was responsible for which jockey's first Group 1 success when winning the Diamond Jubilee Stakes at Royal Ascot in 2013?

8. Who was aboard Sir Mark Prescott's filly Marsha when she took the honours in the 2017 Nunthorpe Stakes?

9. Who partnered Henry Candy's Markab when he was successful in the 2010 running of the Haydock Sprint Cup?

10. This 'new kid on the block' gave Gifted Master a great ride to get up to win the Stewards' Cup at Goodwood for trainer Hugo Palmer in 2018. Who is he?

QUIZ No 28

CURRENT JOCKEYS – JUMPS.

1. Which jockey concluded 2018 by landing the Long Walk Hurdle at Ascot on Emma Lavelle's Paisley Park, before winning the Stayers' Hurdle at the Cheltenham Festival in 2019 on the same horse.

2. Previous to Davy Russell's Aintree exploits in 2018 and 2019, who was the last jockey to ride consecutive Grand National winners?

3. In the entire history of Cheltenham's Queen Mother Champion Chase there has been only one instance of a father and son combination winning the race as trainer and jockey. Who were the two men involved?

4. Trainer Gordon Elliott landed his first Cheltenham Gold Cup in 2016 when Don Cossack triumphed. Who rode him?

5. When Lord Windermere produced his 20-1 Cheltenham Gold Cup shock in 2014 it made Jim Culloty the only man this century to both ride and train a Gold Cup winner. Who helped him from the saddle in this achievement?

6. Which jockey's CV includes a Grand National for Gordon Elliott and a Cheltenham Gold Cup for Jessica Harrington?

7. The 2010 Cheltenham Gold Cup was billed as a match between Denman and Kauto Star but one jockey had other ideas and pinched the race aboard Imperial Commander. Who was he?

8. Which jockey won two bet365 Gold Cups in three years at Sandown with Just A Par for Paul Nicholls in 2015 and Henllan Harri for Peter Bowen in 2017?

9. Who rode the Bob Buckler-trained Niche Market when he won the Irish Grand National in 2009?

10. Alan King landed his first and so far only Scottish Grand National with Godsmejudge in 2013. Who got it over the line?

CURRENT TRAINERS – FLAT.

1. Which Richard Hannon – snr or jnr – trained Sky Lantern when, ridden by Richard Hughes, she won the 2013 1,000 Guineas?

2. Pastoral Pursuits in 2005 and Sakhee's Secret in 2007 were winners of the July Cup for which trainer?

3. Which trainer had a 25-1 Ebor Handicap winner in 2011 when Dale Swift drove Moyenne Corniche home on the Knavesmire?

4. Which trainer landed a big fish when Cross Counter took the 2018 Melbourne Cup for Godolphin under Kerrin McEvoy?

5. Which Newmarket trainer won his, to date, only Classic when Kingston Hill, with Andrea Atzeni doing the steering, won the 2014 St Leger?

6. Which trainer entered the record books in August 2018 when, as a result of Frankie Dettori's win aboard Poet's Society at York, he reached 4,194 winners; more than any previous British trainer?

7. Ribchester winning the 2017 Queen Anne Stakes at Royal Ascot contributed to this trainer's total of 30 Group wins. Who is he?

8. Daryll Holland, Frankie Dettori and Neil Callan were the three jockeys involved when Halmaheera won Doncaster's Portland Handicap three years running from 2002. Which trainer was responsible for this achievement?

9. Which trainer in the 21st century has won the Oaks twice but, as of 2019, has drawn a blank in the other four British Classics?

10. Which two trainers since the mid-1990s have done the Derby and Oaks double without, so far, winning any other British Classic?

CURRENT TRAINERS – JUMPS.

1. Who is the only current jumps trainer to have ridden and trained a winner on the Flat, over hurdles and over fences at Ascot?

2. Which trainer, on October 26, 2018, with Sam Red at Cheltenham, became the fastest to record 100 winners in a season, breaking Martin Pipe's 17-year-old record?

3. Who, in 2015 and 2016, trained the winner of Kempton's King George VI Chase with two different horses?

4. As of 2019, who is the only current trainer to have won the Grand National both before and after 2000?

5. Who trained Diamond Harry to win the 2010 Hennessy Gold Cup at Newbury, partnered by Daryl Jacob?

6. Which trainer won the Welsh Grand National in 2009 when Tom O'Brien got home first on Dream Alliance?

7. God's Own's victory in the 2016 Melling Chase, ridden by Paddy Brennan, was an Aintree win for which trainer?

8. Which current trainer did the Champion Hurdle and Gold Cup double in 1995 with Alderbrook and Master Oats?

9. When Cole Harden sprang a 14-1 surprise by winning Cheltenham's World Hurdle in 2015 it was a big boost to the career of which trainer?

10. Unowhatimeanharry provided which trainer with a Cheltenham Festival win in the Albert Bartlett Novices' Hurdle of 2016?

'DISTAFF.'

All these fillies are Classic winners with female names

1. Married woman wins the 1977 1,000 Guineas for Mick Easterby and Eddie Hide.

2. Oaks success for Dick Hern and Willie Carson at Epsom in 1983.

3. Lose the 'Lady' but why was she spotted on a horse in Coventry when she should have been at Newmarket landing the Guineas and Oaks double in 1940?

4. Sounds like an impoverished housewife but it was the successful filly in the 1980 running of the French Oaks for trainer Ian Balding and jockey Lester Piggott.

5. Victorious in the 1996 Oaks for jockey Pat Eddery and trainer Henry Cecil, it sounds as though the barmaid from Cheers has been putting on airs!

6. A raid on the French Oaks proves successful for trainer Paul Kelleway and jockey Lester Piggott in 1981.

7. A big moment in the careers of trainer Ben Hanbury and jockey Ray Cochrane as this filly did the double in 1986, taking both the 1,000 Guineas and the Oaks.

8. Keep it under your hat but trainer Sir Mark Prescott and jockey Seb Sanders have won the 2006 French Oaks.

9. Filly that likes to get up close with water in her leisure time takes the Oaks at Epsom in 1991 for trainer Jim Bolger and jockey Christy Roche.

10. Sounds like a 1970s song by David Soul but she won the French Oaks in 1989 for trainer Roger Wojtowiez and jockey Tony Cruz.

'FLAT HUNTING.'

A few questions on the growing phenomenon of jumps trainers targeting the top staying Flat races.

1. One jumps trainer has had winners in all four of the following races. Who is he? The Cesarewitch, Chester Cup, Ascot Stakes and Queen Alexandra Stakes.

2. Which jumps trainer won Ascot's Queen Alexandra Stakes in both 2016 and 2018 with Commissioned and Pallasator?

3. Which jumps trainer took the Chester Cup in successive seasons, in 2011 and 2012, with Overturn and Ile De Re?

4. In 2006, this horse, trained by Philip Hobbs and ridden by Richard Johnson, won the Triumph Hurdle at Cheltenham before later that year winning the Cesarewitch under Jamie Spencer. Who was he?

5. Nicky Henderson's Caracciola, in 2008 and 2009, won three Flat races, a victory at York being sandwiched between wins in the 2008 Cesarewitch at Newmarket and the 2009 Queen Alexandra Stakes at Ascot. Who were the two successful jockeys involved in these three wins?

6. The Ascot Stakes has been a favourite target. Jumps trainers have plundered it 16 times in the last 27 years. Which Charles Byrnes-trained, Fran Berry-ridden horse summed up their control of the race when winning it in 2014?

7. Grumeti was a shock winner of the Cesarewitch in 2015 when, under Adam Beschizza, he triumphed at odds of 50-1. Who trained it?

8. The attack on the plums of the Flat tree began a long time ago. Which trainer won the Ascot Stakes in 1993 and 1994 with Balasani and Sweet Glow?

9. Recently, Willie Mullins has had great success in farming the Ascot Stakes, winning it four times since 2012 with Simenon, Clondaw Warrior, Thomas Hobson and Lagostovegas. The first three were ridden by Ryan Moore. Who rode the last one?

10. Which trainer produced Mamlook to win the Chester Cup in 2010 under Richard Hughes?

FLOWERS AND PLANTS.

All these horses' names contain flowers or plants.

1. This plant with blue, white or pink flowers constituted Vincent O'Brien's first Derby winner in 1962.

2. This brilliant filly achieved the relatively rare feat of winning successive King George VI and Queen Elizabeth Stakes at Ascot in 1973 and 1974 for French trainer Maurice Zilber, the first under Bill Pyers, the second under Lester Piggott.

3. Winner of the 2018 Lockinge Stakes at Newbury for Aidan O'Brien and Ryan Moore.

4. This shrub provided the first word of the horse that won the 2007 Northumberland Plate for jockey Luke Morris and trainer Michael Bell.

5. Winner of the 2005 Dubai World Cup at Nad Al Sheba for trainer Dale Romans and jockey John Velasquez.

6. This four-time winner of Kempton's King George VI Chase is possibly the most loved racehorse of all.

7. Male version of a plant that can double as a soft cheese! He was successful for trainer Walter Bentley and jockey Willie Higgins in the 1979 Ayr Gold Cup.

8. A career-best performance and a defeat of the brilliant Baracouda in the Stayers' Hurdle at the Cheltenham Festival in 2004 could be seen as a present for Barry Geraghty and Jonjo O'Neill.

9. The biggest win for this Aidan O'Brien-trained, Ryan Moore-ridden filly came at Ascot in October 2017 when she prevailed in the prestigious British Champions Fillies and Mares Stakes.

10. A plant whose flowers grow in clusters turned out to be an exceptionally quick sprinter when winning the 1960 New Stakes at Ascot and then taking York's Nunthorpe Stakes the next year, both times for jockey Ron Hutchinson and trainer Paddy Prendergast.

FOOTBALL.

1. Which popular winner of Cheltenham's 2012 Centenary Novices' Handicap Chase contains the names of two players from England's 1966 World Cup winning team?

2. Best Mate's colours, selected by owner Jim Lewis, were chosen to represent which football club?

3. The Queen's horse, trained by Dick Hern and ridden by Joe Mercer, that won the 1971 Henry II Stakes at Sandown, could have been named after two footballing brothers or a football club. What was the horse called?

4. Wilfried Zaha is the current example of this Jack Berry-trained winner of Ascot's Wokingham Stakes in both 1997 and 1998.

5. It was quite some feat for this Premier League club to land the Sussex Stakes of 1886, 19 years before the club came into existence!

6. The Royal Hunt Cup winner of 1985, trained by Clive Brittain and ridden by Chris Rutter, is a cry often heard at the King Power, Goodison, Stamford Bridge, Portman Road and St Andrew's grounds.

7. This football club, which lost its league status in 2018, won the 1892 Doncaster Cup and is also a now defunct Goodwood race, a cigarette and something to sit on if you feel tired!

8. This 66-1 winner of the 1963 Grand National has recently been the rock at the heart of Middlesbrough's defence.

9. This horse, named after the scorer of the winning goal for Arsenal in the 1971 FA Cup Final was trained by Peter Robinson at Newmarket and won races in 1972, 1973 and 1974.

10. Legendary Real Madrid player who was a worthy favourite when landing the 2007 running of the Stewards' Cup at Goodwood, its rider and trainer being Jamie Spencer and James Fanshawe.

FRENCH JOCKEYS.

1. Who is the only French jockey to win both the 1,000 Guineas and 2,000 Guineas this century?

2. Who is the only post-war French jockey to have won all five British Classics?

3. Which French jockey, riding Pour Moi in the 2011 Derby, celebrated his victory by standing up in the irons before he had hit the front?

4. Which French jockey won the Derby in 1961 for trainer Harry Wragg on Psidium at 66-1?

5. Which French jockey won the Derby in the last century and the 2,000 Guineas in this century?

6. Which French jockey, currently riding in Britain, is the only man in modern times to win three successive French Oaks between 1997 and 1999?

7. Which French jockey took the 2,000 Guineas in 1995 on the very smart colt Pennekamp?

8. Which French jockey won the St Leger in 1979 on Son Of Love for French trainer Robert Collet?

9. Which French jockey was victorious in the 1983 running of the 1,000 Guineas on Ma Biche and then won it again with the very talented Miesque in 1987?

10. Which French jockey guided Miss France to win the 1,000 Guineas of 2014?

HISTORICAL FIGURES.

1. Most certainly the only Prime Minister, in 1881, to win the November Handicap while in office.

2. While on the year 1881 this horse, named after a United States President assassinated in that year, won the 2017 Mill Reef Stakes, trained by George Scott and ridden by Frankie Dettori.

3. Unlucky horse named for an English hero, trained by Aidan O'Brien and ridden by Kieren Fallon. The horse lost his life in the 2006 Derby.

4. He may have won Redcar's Zetland Gold Cup in 1994 under Gary Hind for John Gosden but this walker and writer would have been much happier about 90 miles west.

5. Nineteenth century English soldier murdered in Khartoum in 1885 but somehow managed to land the Chester Vase 81 years later for trainer Jack Jarvis and jockey Paul Cook.

6. Whether we take Richard Hannon snr's excellent charge of recent years or Gordon Richards's winning ride in the 1933 Chester Cup, this highwayman, like not a few horses, came to grief on the Knavesmire.

7. Without the efforts of this 15th century pioneer you might not be looking at this question that asks you who won the Cambridgeshire in 1940, when it was run at Nottingham?

8. Extremely significant 19th century Irish politician who stayed on to win the 1971 running of Royal Ascot's Queen's Vase under Aussie jockey Ron Hutchinson.

9. Synonymous with 18th century furniture, the equine version won the 2012 King Edward VII Stakes at Royal Ascot, trained by Henry Cecil and ridden by Johnny Murtagh.

10. This fifth century BC long distance runner probably found the six furlongs of the Gimcrack Stakes too short for him in 1957 but he triumphed nevertheless, with trainer Captain Charles Elsey and jockey Doug Smith in supporting roles.

THE KING GEORGE VI AND QUEEN ELIZABETH STAKES.

1. Since its inception in 1951 which trainer has won the race the most times?

2. Who was the only horse in the 1970s to win both the King George and Prix de l'Arc de Triomphe in the same year?

3. In the last century, 14 horses won the King George after having taken the Derby. So far this century only one has done so. Who?

4. Which jockey has won the race the most times?

5. Danedream, the winner in 2012, was the first to be trained in which country? They won it the next year, too!

6. Who is the only jockey this century to ride two odds-on winners of the King George?

7. If you looked at the result of the 2015 edition of the King George why might you be forgiven for thinking that the race didn't take place?

8. Who are the only two horses this century to win the Arc in the same year that they won the King George?

9. Who are the only two trainers to saddle three successive winners of the King George? It happened from 1966 to 1968 and again from 1997 to 1999.

10. The shortest priced winner of the race at odds of 2-9 was successful for trainer Dick Hern and jockey Willie Carson in 1989. What was the horse called?

QUIZ No 38

LINKS.

1. What links the following racecourses? Stratford, Warwick, Newbury and Leicester.

2. Besides having been National Hunt jockeys what else links Dick Francis, John Francome and Tony McCoy?

3. Stockwell, Kingsway, Pall Mall and Roland Gardens are all places in London. What else links them?

4. How are the following jockeys linked? Graham Bradley, David Goulding, Jonjo O'Neill, Robert Earnshaw and Dermot Browne.

5. What links the following four Classic winners? Reference Point, Doyoun, Fairy Footsteps and Shirley Heights.

6. What links the following four jumps courses? Cheltenham, Wincanton, Plumpton and Towcester.

7. What links the following three Derby winners? Golden Fleece (1982), Secreto (1984) and Galileo (2001).

8. What links the following three horses? Tag, Pia and Was.

9. Which one of the five Classics have the following jockeys all won? Joe Mercer, Eddie Hide, Walter Swinburn, Richard Hills, Kieren Fallon, Richard Hughes and Johnny Murtagh.

10. What links the following four horses? Larbawn, Diamond Edge, Topsham Bay and Ad Hoc.

LITERATURE. PART ONE – BOOKS.

1. In 1878 a Shakespeare play won Ascot's Royal Hunt Cup but, by all accounts, the race was run in June, not the middle of March!

2. The winner of the 1972 Cesarewitch for jockey Taffy Thomas and trainer Staff Ingham was a well-known Laurie Lee novel.

3. Sired by Royal Applause and trained by Dandy Nicholls, this horse won two small races at Carlisle and Beverley in 2008 and shares its name with the first Julian Barnes novel.

4. A nine-time winner, this Jeremy Hindley-trained speedball was a top two-year old of 1972. It derived its name from the previous year's film starring Alan Bates and Julie Christie, based on a novel by L.P. Hartley.

5. This horse, named for arguably F Scott Fitzgerald's greatest work, finished second under Pat Eddery in Kris Kin's Derby of 2003.

6. Trained by Jack Fawcus and ridden by Walter Bentley, this horse won the Zetland Gold Cup at Redcar in 1956 and was named after a famous Charles Dickens novel on the French Revolution.

7. The location for Chaucer's Tales, this horse, trained by Vincent O'Brien and ridden by Bill Williamson, landed the 1969 Doncaster Cup.

8. Jeremy Tree and Joe Mercer combined to win the King's Stand Stakes at Royal Ascot in 1968. The winner's name was the family name in the title of a much-loved Thomas Hardy novel.

9. This horse, which could have been named after James Joyce's modernist 1922 masterpiece, was an impressive winner of both the Eclipse Stakes and International Stakes in 2017, under the guidance of Sir Michael Stoute.

10. The novelistic account of the horrors of schooling in 19th century England by Charles Dickens provided the name of the 50-1 winner of Ascot's Royal Hunt Cup of 1955, trained by Fred Armstrong and ridden by Willie Snaith.

LITERATURE. PART TWO – WRITERS.

1. Twentieth century poet who provided the name for the Aidan O'Brien-trained, Kieren Fallon-ridden winner of the 2007 Arc.

2. Irish colt ridden by Tony Murray and trained by Mick O'Toole who triumphed in the Eclipse Stakes after finishing second to the mighty Troy in both the British and Irish Derbys of 1979. Not initially named after the most famous novelist of the 19th century but an early change of one letter meant that he eventually was.

3. Liverpool legend or Irish poet, they would both have been proud to have this four-time Ascot Gold Cup winner named after them.

4. Newmarket trainer Sir Mark Prescott gained the second of his three Cambridgeshire Handicap victories in 1997 when George Duffield got home on this Russian who penned Doctor Zhivago.

5. This Anglo-Irish playwright and novelist served some time in prison but it didn't stop him winning the 1958 Welsh Grand National.

6. This winner of the 1886 running of the Goodwood Cup is still used to this day as an alternative title for William Shakespeare.

7. In 2012, this Belgian writer of detective stories, partnered by Ryan Moore and trained in Ireland by Willie Mullins, won both the Ascot Stakes and the Queen Alexandra Stakes at the royal meeting.

8. This famous playboy English poet won Newbury's Mill Reef Stakes in 2003 for jockey Jamie Spencer and trainer David Loder.

9. In 1936 this horse upset the odds in the St Leger and then upset them again in the following year's Eclipse Stakes, on both occasions being returned at 20-1. In his spare time, when things were quiet at the stable, he also managed to find time to write a magnificent account of the life of Samuel Johnson!

10. An even-money victor in the 2,000 Guineas of 1932, though it would have been more appropriate if he had won it 52 years later!

QUIZ No 41. 'LOCATION, LOCATION, LOCATION' – PART ONE. THE FLAT.

Where are the following races held?

1. The Old Newton Cup.

2. The Portland Handicap.

3. The Nell Gwyn Stakes.

4. The Winter Hill Stakes.

5. The Great St Wilfrid Handicap.

6. The Lonsdale Stakes.

7. The Woodcote Stakes.

8. The Zetland Gold Cup.

9. The Cocked Hat Stakes.

10. The Lily Agnes Stakes.

'LOCATION, LOCATION, LOCATION' – PART TWO. JUMPS.

Where are the following races held?

1. The Welsh Grand National.

2. The Challow Hurdle.

3. The Eider Chase.

4. The Long Walk Hurdle.

5. The Peterborough Chase.

6. The Irish Grand National.

7. The Imperial Cup.

8. The Kingwell Hurdle.

9. The Cleeve Hurdle.

10. The Charlie Hall Chase.

LOOSE LETTERS.

1. Add one letter to the end of the jockey who won Ascot's King George VI and Queen Elizabeth Stakes in 2012 on Danedream and produce the jockey who won the same race 30 years earlier on Kalaglow. Who are the two jockeys?

2. A tough one! In 1962 Harmon won the Portland Handicap at Doncaster. Its Yorkshire based trainer and the champion jockey who rode it had nearly the same name, the jockey having one extra letter near the start of his name. Who were they?

3. Add one letter to the front of the horse that won the 2017 running of the Dubai World Cup at Meydan and produce a Yorkshire town. Name the horse and town.

4. Place three letters in the middle of the horse that won the 2016 Grand National and produce the winner of the 2013 Derby. Which are the two horses?

5. Remove the last letter from what is often chanted at Leeds, Newcastle and West Ham to produce the 1987 Oaks winner. What was its name?

6. Add one letter to the front of an ungelded horse to produce the winner of Ascot's King George in 1996.

7. Take two letters from the front of an Italian football club to produce the winner of the 2001 running of the St Leger. Name the club and the horse.

8. Add one letter to the front of an English playwright murdered in the 1960s to produce the jockey that rode the Oaks winner of 1969. Name them both.

9. Take one letter from the end of the Nicky Henderson-trained and Barry Geraghty-ridden horse who took the 2008 Long Walk Hurdle at Ascot and produce a racecourse. Name the horse and the course.

10. Add one letter to a sign of the Zodiac to produce the winner of the 2005 St Leger. Name them both.

THE LETTER 'M' IN THE ST LEGER.

Between 1900 and 1985 only one winner of Doncaster's St Leger began with the letter 'M.' Then, as if to make good the imbalance, they started arriving like London buses, nine turning up in the ensuing 26 years. Their dates and connections are given below. Can you name the horses?

	Date	Jockey	Trainer	Owner	Odds
1.	1986	P. Eddery	J. Dunlop	Duchess of Norfolk	9-2
2.	1988	W. Carson	N. Graham	Lady Beaverbrook	15-2
3.	1989	S. Cauthen	H. Cecil	Charles St George	6-4
4.	1994	P. Eddery	B. Hills	Sheikh Mohammed	40-1
5.	1999	R. Hills	Saeed Bin Suroor	Godolphin	11-2
6.	2000	T. Quinn	J. Dunlop	Neil Jones	11-4
7.	2001	M. Kinane	A. O'Brien	Mrs J. Magnier/M. Tabor	13-8
8.	2009	T. Durcan	Saeed Bin Suroor	Godolphin	14-1
9.	2011	W. Buick	J. Gosden	Bjorn Nielsen	15-2

10. To complete the ten, which highly talented filly, in 1955, was the only other 'M' to win the race in the 20th century? She was completing the fillies' Triple Crown, having already taken the 1,000 Guineas and Oaks.

QUIZ No 45. THE MISSING WORD ROUND – PART ONE. FLAT RACING.

Enter a new word in the space to produce two horses. For example, King's (Best) Mate.

1. Brown .... Hobbs

2. Soviet .... Appeal

3. North .... Cavalry

4. Jupiter .... Sands

5. Midway .... Carla

6. Law .... Rock

7. Long .... Here

8. Celtic .... Easy

9. Take .... Up

10. Colour .... Cecil

QUIZ No 46

THE MISSING WORD ROUND – PART TWO. JUMP RACING.

1. Nicolaus .... Buck

2. Imperial .... Equiname

3. Tied .... Rake

4. Viking .... Uberalles

5. Cool .... Run

6. Charter .... Politics

7. Teeton .... House

8. The Young .... Minded

9. Long .... And Skip

10. Sea .... Island

THE MISSING WORD ROUND – PART THREE.

Enter a new word in the space to produce two jockeys, trainers or owners.

1. Peter   ....   Bunker Hunt

2. Tom   ....   Duffield

3. Ron   ....   Hills

4. Willie   ....   Moore

5. Dave   ....   Hern

6. Tony   ....   Dwyer

7. Henry   ....   Boyd-Rochfort

8. Duncan   ....   Dalgleish

9. Bruce   ....   Guest

10. Robert   ....   Churchill

QUIZ No 48

'MOONING' (Tastefully of course).

All the horses have 'Moon' in their name.

1. You can more easily catch your prey if the sky contains the 1940 Cesarewitch winner, trained by Fred Darling and ridden by Gordon Richards.

2. Filly successful in the 2008 running of the Irish Oaks for Aidan O'Brien and Johnny Murtagh.

3. John Dunlop and Willie Carson were the fortunate trainer and jockey when this horse won the Goodwood Cup for the Duchess of Norfolk in 1990.

4. Winner of the prestigious Dubai World Cup at Meydan in 2003 for Frankie Dettori and Godolphin.

5. Possibly named after a great Little Feat song, this horse won the Group 1 Prix de Saint-Cloud in 2009 for Khalid Abdullah, Ryan Moore and Sir Michael Stoute.

6. A 33-1 upset in Epsom's Great Metropolitan Handicap of 1967, trained by Ken Cundell and ridden by Tony Murray.

7. Another Sir Michael Stoute and Ryan Moore victory, this time in Royal Ascot's Hardwicke Stakes in 2012.

8. He failed to scale the heights when finishing fourth in Blakeney's 1969 Derby, when ridden by Yves Saint-Martin and trained by Vincent O'Brien. However, he did finish in front of the Lester Piggott-ridden Ribofilio, the favourite to win the race.

9. This Richard Hannon jnr-trained horse provided jockey Pat Dobbs with his first Group 1 success when the son of Dylan Thomas won Epsom's Coronation Cup in 2015 for owner John Manley.

10. This Ebor Handicap winner at York in 2007 was obviously going through a good patch at the time for trainer Luca Cumani and jockey Jamie Spencer!

NATIONALITIES.

The first word of all the answers refers to a national identity. For example, Chinese Cracker, English Prince.

1. Ron Hutchinson and trainer John Dunlop landed Sandown's Eclipse Stakes in 1973 with a weapon from north of the border. What was it?

2. This 1978 Champion Stakes winner for jockey Greville Starkey and trainer Paul Kelleway was also a big hit for Del Shannon in the early 1960s.

3. Sadler's Wells-sired, Sir Michael Stoute-trained colt who, in 1999 and 2000, finished runner-up in no fewer than five Group 1 races.

4. Winner of the Royal Hunt Cup at Ascot in 2013 when ridden by James Doyle and trained by George Baker.

5. Named after a Roman landmark, this horse lived up to his owner-trainer's name by winning the 1969 Hennessy Gold Cup and then being placed in three successive Grand Nationals.

6. After finishing third in Mill Reef's Derby this French colt bounced back a month later to appropriately win another Derby.

7. Highly talented grey associated with Henry Cecil and Steve Cauthen who took the 1988 Champion Stakes in fine style.

8. Sandy Barclay and Geoff Lewis were the pilots when this Jim Joel-owned and Noel Murless-trained colt achieved the relatively rare distinction of landing Newbury's Lockinge Stakes in successive years, namely 1970 and 1971.

9. Lovely Cheveley Park filly who triumphed in the 2003 1,000 Guineas under Kieren Fallon for Sir Michael Stoute.

10. Trained by Peter Chapple-Hyam he was the top British two-year-old of 2006 when unbeaten in four races. As a three-year-old he finished third in the 2,000 Guineas and second in the July Cup. What was his name?

NO MEAN FEAT.

Trainers who have run up impressive sequences.

1. Which trainer ran up a sequence of 10 wins in a row with Spindrifter in 1980, the horse ending up with a race in his honour at Pontefract?

2. Which trainer won the Irish Derby seven times in succession between 2006 and 2012?

3. Which trainer won Royal Ascot's Queen's Vase four consecutive times between 1963 and 1966 with Hereford, I Titan, Beddard and Bally Russe?

4. One of the great feats in racing history is this trainer's seven successive Irish Grand Nationals between 1960 and 1966. Who was he?

5. In the early years of this century which trainer took the Ayr Gold Cup six times in 11 years, twice with Funfair Wane and, at one point, having four winners in five runnings of the race?

6. Vinnie Roe, ridden by Pat Smullen, won four successive Irish St Legers between 2001 and 2004 under the guidance of which trainer?

7. From its inception in 1963, Newbury's Schweppes Gold Trophy was won in four of its first five seasons by one trainer who shared his wins with three horses; Rosyth on two occasions, Le Vermontois and Hill House. Josh Gifford was the ever-present jockey. Who was the trainer?

8. Before falling out with Golden Miller's owner, Dorothy Paget, who trained the great horse for the first four of his five Cheltenham Gold Cup wins between 1932 and 1935?

9. Between 2000 and 2005, the exceptional staying hurdler Baracouda won four Long Walk Hurdles and two World Hurdles. In his nine appearances in these two races he was never out of the first two. Some record! Who trained him?

10. In August 2018 Roy Rocket won the Kew Electrical Handicap at Brighton. It was the grey gelding's ninth win at the track and he became something of a cult hero beside the seaside. Who trains him?

OCCUPATIONS.

All these horses are also jobs.

1. Whether he was dealing in candles or ships' supplies he won the 1848 Grand National.

2. We've all had a horse get stuffed once in a while but look no further than this 1958 winner of the Hennessy Gold Cup and Whitbread Gold Cup to see how it's done!

3. This labourer won the 1895 running of the Northumberland Plate but containerisation in the second half of the 20th century has reduced his numbers and power.

4. In ancient Rome he was responsible for 100 men but he still found time to land the 1978 Cesarewitch for trainer Ian Balding and jockey John Matthias.

5. You might take your boots to this winner of Ascot's Coventry Stakes in 1947, when ridden by Gordon Richards and trained by Fred Darling.

6. You can never find one of these when you want one but it's not surprising this one was nowhere to be found as he was in France winning their Derby for jockey Willie Carson and trainer Charlie Milbank in 1980.

7. Ancient pharmacist wins the 1915 Ascot Gold Cup.

8. Not sure who won Doncaster's Portland Handicap in 1938. It could have been Ringo Starr, Charlie Watts or Ginger Baker!

9. The 1964 City and Suburban Handicap at Epsom was a much bigger deal then than it is now and it was won for owner Lord Rosebery by trainer Jack Jarvis and jockey Stan Smith with a horse whose name is a nautical shorthand for the man in charge of a ship's crew.

10. Clearly, there are two different horses involved here but they share the same name and underwater occupation! The first was placed in the 1868 and 1871 Grand Nationals while the second won the 1947 Derby. Roy Orbison sings about one in his song 'Leah.'

ODD ONE OUT.

Which is the odd one out in the following?

1. Red Rum – Red Splash – Red Alligator – Red Marauder.

2. Which one of the following jockeys has not won the Flat jockeys' title? Michael Roberts – Walter Swinburn – Kevin Darley – Joe Mercer.

3. Which racecourse is the odd one out? Epsom – Ascot – Doncaster – Newmarket.

4. Which jockey is the odd one out? Doug Smith – Joe Mercer – Willie Carson – Pat Eddery – Richard Hills.

5. Which horse is the odd one out? Snow Marten – Snow Knight – Snow Bride – Snow Fairy.

6. Which is the odd horse out of these winners of the Irish Derby? Soldier Of Fortune – Treasure Beach – Frozen Fire – Capri.

The final four questions concern the following top trainers: John Gosden, Sir Michael Stoute, Barry Hills and Sir Henry Cecil. Each of them is the odd man out in one of the four questions. Who is it each time, at least until the end of 2019?

7. Who has not trained a winner of the Prix de l'Arc de Triomphe?

8. Who has not trained a Derby winner?

9. Who has not trained a 2,000 Guineas winner?

10. Who is the only one to have trained the winner of a Champion Hurdle?

PAINTERS.

1. Described by Aidan O'Brien as the fastest horse he had ever trained, this colt remained unbeaten in four starts as a two-year-old, his wins including Royal Ascot's Coventry Stakes. In 2017 he took the Commonwealth Cup at the same venue but lost his form afterwards and failed to win again.

2. This 20th century Swiss painter and sculptor won the 1973 running of Doncaster's Champagne Stakes and York's Gimcrack Stakes for jockey Tony Murray and trainer Ryan Price. In 1974 he went on to win the Champion Stakes.

3. This horse, named after a key figure in the Vienna Secession Movement of the early 20th century, trained by Aidan O'Brien and ridden by his son Donnacha, finished runner-up to Without Parole in the 2018 edition of the St. James's Palace Stakes at Ascot.

4. Lady James Douglas, in 1918, became the first woman to own a Derby winner when which horse that shares its name with a great 18th century English landscape and portrait painter was the odds-on victor in the race?

5. In the 16th century he produced an iconic portrait of Henry VIII and was no slouch on the racecourse either, winning the 2015 Chester Vase for Aidan O'Brien and Ryan Moore.

6. This French painter, who died in 1947, came back to life to land the 1962 Doncaster Cup for trainer Jack Clayton and jockey Ron Hutchinson. The artist was the subject of a major London exhibition in 2019.

7. Many judges reckon this 17th century Spanish master to be the best there was and he was some horse too, winning the 1897 Champion Stakes and repeating the dose the following year, when he also took the Eclipse Stakes.

8. Responsible for 'The Birth of Venus', he still found time to win the Ascot Gold Cup in 1955 under Italian jockey Enrico Camici.

9. French Impressionist impresses by winning the Stewards' Cup in 1960, ridden by Jimmy Lindley and trained by Jeremy Tree.

10. Probably the most influential painter of the 20th century, he didn't need his surname to tell everyone he had won the 2003 Lincoln Handicap when trained by Barry Hills and ridden by his son Michael.

QUIZ No 54

POT LUCK.

1. Ginger McCain trained this Liverpool footballer's horse, Wayward Scot, for the 1979 Grand National but the player was unable to see it run because he was playing in an FA Cup semi-final against Manchester United. The horse fell and so, after a replay, did Liverpool. Who owned the horse?

2. Which future television presenter was on board when Cool Ground won the Welsh Grand National for trainer Reg Akehurst in 1990?

3. Kieren Fallon's six Flat jockeys' titles came in two groups of three. Which jockey, by winning the 2000 title, denied Fallon winning seven in a row between 1997 and 2003?

4. Walter Swinburn in 1987 and Ryan Moore in 2019 have both completed back-to-back July Cup victories. Between these dates who is the only other jockey to achieve this double? (Clue: he did it with Pastoral Pursuits in 2005 and Les Arcs in 2006).

5. When Harbour Law won the 2016 St Leger under jockey George Baker which woman became the first of her sex to train the winner of the race?

6. In the 1866 Grand National two consecutive playing cards ran in the race, both of them falling. People have been known to wear the suit on their sleeves. What were the two horses called?

7. Up until 2018, five jockeys this century have won both the Cambridgeshire and the Cesarewitch. How many can you name?

8. Which three female trainers have won the Scottish Grand National this century? The successful horses were Gingembre in 2001, Wayward Prince in 2015 and Joe Farrell in 2018.

9. The 'Epsom Dash' was won by the same horse in 2014, 2016 and 2017. What was odd about it was that it involved three different jockeys and three different trainers. What was the horse called?

10. In the 1997 running of Sandown's Tingle Creek Chase the winning horse, ridden by Russ Garritty, shared part of his name with the first name of the trainer. What were horse and trainer called?

RACECOURSE PUZZLERS. PART ONE – THE NORTH AND SCOTLAND.

Identify the following racecourses.

1. The only racecourse to score a goal in an FA Cup Final. It happened in 2014.

2. Ferrari.

3. Australian city.

4. Tony Blair's constituency.

5. Richard II died in mysterious circumstances in the castle of this town in 1400.

6. The only racecourse with three letters.

7. Everton manager who guided them to league titles in 1963 and 1970 and victory in the FA Cup in 1966.

8. Alison Steadman played this character in the first production of Mike Leigh's play 'Abigail's Party'.

9. Take away the first two letters of an Essex town.

10. Tickets were hard to come by for this American show when it reached London's West End in 2017.

RACECOURSE PUZZLERS. PART TWO – THE SOUTH AND IRELAND.

Identify the following racecourses.

1. Successful trainer of Foinavon, winner of the much talked about Grand National of 1967.

2. Something you might want after strenuous exertion.

3. Humorous poem of five lines.

4. Anagram of well-known Puccini opera.

5. It's a long way to this course!

6. You might get the water required for the first part from the second part!

7. Card game.

8. Viv Richards and Ian Botham used to star here.

9. The only palindromic racecourse.

10. Isle of Wight town.

REDS.

All these horses have the word 'Red' in their name.

1. Did the waves figuratively part to allow this Richard Quinn-ridden and Paul Cole-trained horse to take Ascot's Coventry Stakes in 1998?

2. You were warned that this horse, ridden by Johnny Roe and trained by Dermot Weld, would land Goodwood's Stewards' Cup in 1974!

3. Nobody could hold one of these to this Jimmy Fox-ridden and Ricky Vallance-trained winner of the 1973 Hennessy Gold Cup.

4. Usually sent to a humanitarian crisis, this horse, produced by Pat Eddery and Peter Walwyn, won Newbury's Mill Reef Stakes in 1974.

5. Perhaps Martin Dwyer and Jamie Osborne had a celebratory glass after the November Handicap of 2002.

6. 2007 and Newbury proved to be the time and place for the winner of both the Lockinge Stakes and Hungerford Stakes for Jamie Spencer and Michael Bell.

7. Royal Hunt Cup victory in 1997 for Olivier Peslier and Reg Akehurst.

8. Sounds like a military affair for Robert Miles and Richard Price as they land the 2004 Chester Vase.

9. A consistent, brave sort, this horse won the Coventry Stakes in 2005 and, as a four-year-old, captured the Haydock Sprint Cup for Michael and Barry Hills.

10. His dad was Quorum and his mum was Mared. He cost 400 guineas and on April 7, 1967 dead-heated in a five-furlong selling race for two-year-olds. How does he justify his place in this quiz?

REGAL BEASTS.

All these horses begin with 'Royal'.

1. Incredible Breeders' Cup Mile success for 54-year-old Lester Piggott in 1990.

2. Grand National victory for Jason Titley and Jenny Pitman in 1995.

3. Dual winner of the Ascot Gold Cup in 2001 and 2002 for Johnny Murtagh and Mark Johnston.

4. Graham McCourt and James Fanshawe combined to bring home the Champion Hurdle for Sheikh Mohammed in 1992.

5. This horse, trained by Noel Murless and ridden by Australian George Moore, was victorious in both the 2,000 Guineas and the Derby in 1967.

6. Perhaps the Queen's 1966 Goodwood Cup winner, Gaulois, produced this Taffy Thomas and Bill O'Gorman winner of the 1969 running of the Stewards' Cup!

7. John Burke and Fred Rimell teamed up for this 1976 winner of the Cheltenham Gold Cup.

8. This horse, trained by Henry Cecil and ridden by American jockey Gary Stevens, won the Juddmonte International Stakes by eight lengths in 1999.

9. Won the 1972 and 1974 runnings of Cheltenham's two-mile Champion Chase before it became the Queen Mother Champion Chase. Trained by Edward Courage and ridden by Bill Smith, it is always one of these for rulers when an heir arrives.

10. Put your hands together for this unbeaten two-year-old who, aged four, trained by Barry Hills and ridden by his son Michael, won the 1997 Haydock Sprint Cup.

ROCK/POP/JAZZ/BLUES.

1. Django Reinhardt and Stephane Grappelli could claim to be this winner of Ascot's Victoria Cup of 2006 for Ryan Moore and David Barron.

2. A track on the 'Aja' album by Steely Dan in 1977 ends up winning the 2011 running of the Wokingham at Royal Ascot, ridden by Johnny Murtagh and trained by James Fanshawe.

3. Back to the Victoria Cup and the winning horse of 1992 is named after Paul McCartney's most convincing solo album, with a little help from Richard Quinn and Bryan McMahon.

4. Highly regarded Oxfordshire-based group who enjoyed great success in the 1990s and provided the name of the winner of the 2009 Norfolk Stakes at Royal Ascot for Jamie Spencer and Brian Meehan.

5. Manfred Mann singer lands the 1958 November Handicap at Doncaster for Arthur Budgett and Joe Mercer.

6. These were designed in America for playing singles on but Lester Piggott won the 1970 Stewards' Cup on one trained by Harold Wallington. Let's face it, he could ride anything!

7. This great band leader and pianist dominated mainstream jazz between the 1920s and 1970s, yet still found time to take Ascot's Victoria Cup in 1977, the year it was run at Newbury. The horse was ridden by Brian Taylor and trained by Ryan Price.

8. Set in New York City and arguably the best of all musicals it also won the 1962 Yorkshire Oaks for trainer Ted Leader and jockey Eph Smith as compensation for being beaten in a photo-finish in the Epsom Oaks.

9. Many youngsters in the 1960s would do this as a prelude to listening to progressive rock bands to enhance their enjoyment. Still do, I guess! But I'm surprised that the name of this winner of the 1989 Scottish Grand National for jockey Brendan Powell and trainer Chris Popham got past the authorities.

10. This grey gelding, named after Pink Floyd's debut single of 1967, ran 22 times over jumps between 2005 and 2011, mostly for trainer Caroline Bailey and jockey Andrew Thornton and won six times. The only time he fell was on the sole occasion that Tony McCoy rode him!

ROYAL ASCOT.

1. On which racecourse was the royal meeting staged in 2005 when Ascot was being redeveloped?

2. Which jockey rode seven winners at the meeting in 1987?

3. It is widely known that, uniquely, Yeats won four successive Gold Cups between 2006 and 2009 but which horse, trained by Jamie Osborne, chased him home on two of the four occasions?

4. Between 1928 and 1934 possibly the most loved horse of all to have run at Royal Ascot won a race at the meeting seven years in a row; a feat unlikely to be equalled. It ensured that his name lives on in a race run annually at Ascot. Who was he?

5. As far as can be known, only one trainer besides Aidan O'Brien with Yeats has won four consecutive Gold Cups. He did it with two horses from 1979 to 1982. Who was he?

6. Master Vote won a particular race at the meeting consecutively in 1947 and 1948 for trainer Herbert Blagrave. In the 175 years of its history this is the only time this has happened. What is the race?

7. What did Stanerra do in 1983 that was repeated by Choisir in 2003, Baddam in 2006, Simenon in 2012 and Blue Point in 2019?

8. Which horse, trained by Edward Lynam, finished third in the 2012 Group 1 King's Stand Stakes before winning it in the next two years with an exhilarating change of gear?

9. Which jockey won the Ascot Gold Cup 11 times between 1957 and 1982?

10. Which horse won the 1973 renewal of the Hardwicke Stakes at the prohibitive odds of 1-5 before a famous win in the Arc later the same year? The odd thing about it was that a French jockey came over to ride him at Ascot and a British jockey went to France to ride him in the Arc!

'SAINTS ALIVE'!

These horses all have St or Saint in their names.

1. West Indian island wins 1871 Portland Handicap at Doncaster.

2. Under Ryan Moore once and Joseph O'Brien twice, this top-class horse won three consecutive Coronation Cups at Epsom between 2011 and 2013 for Joseph's father, Aidan.

3. This winner of the 1840 running of the Ascot Gold Cup was an Italian mystic who lived nearly 800 years ago and in 1980 was made the patron saint of ecology.

4. In 2003 this horse ran out the 20-1 winner of the Ebor Handicap for jockey Richard Quinn and trainer David Elsworth.

5. The 1958 winner of Ascot's Coronation Stakes, trained by Peter Hastings-Bass and ridden by Geoff Lewis can be located just to the north of the answer to question 1.

6. Lester Piggott's third Derby success was on this colt in 1960 for trainer Noel Murless and owner Sir Victor Sassoon.

7. Epsom Coronation Cup winner for Andre Fabre and Pat Eddery in 1986.

8. This winner of the 1885 Coronation Stakes at Ascot was possibly named after an island Napoleon wasn't particularly thrilled to be living on!

9. Lovely stayer for Aidan O'Brien and Ryan Moore who won the Ascot Gold Cup in 2016 before finishing second in the same event the following year.

10. Foaled in 1881, this horse is considered by many to be the greatest of British stallions after siring the winners of 17 Classics. A race named in his honour is run at Newbury each year. Who is he?

SPORT.

1. Able to run very well on two legs, as he demonstrated by recording the first mile in less than four minutes, he managed, on four legs, to win the Gimcrack Stakes at York 46 years later, ably assisted by Johnny Murtagh.

2. Ian Balding and Geoff Lewis conspired to land Ascot's Coventry Stakes in 1968 with an historic rugby stadium.

3. Was Shane Warne in mind when Tony Martin and Johnny Murtagh took the 2007 Cesarewitch?

4. The likes of Phil Taylor, Jocky Wilson and Eric Bristow wouldn't have been able to play without the Gordon Richards-trained winner of the 1966 Dewhurst Stakes who went on to finish third in Royal Palace's Derby.

5. In golf, the venue for handing over the green jacket each year sounds like the winner of an Irish Grand National for Tony McCoy, Jonjo O'Neill and JP McManus.

6. An iconic motor racing circuit in Florida proved good enough to triumph in the 1937 Ayr Gold Cup.

7. It was only fitting that this horse, winner of the Irish Derby in 2015 when in the hands of William Buick for John Gosden, should turn out to be something special because he was named after arguably England's finest opening batsman.

8. A championship golf course and a nice snack before teeing off, it also won the 1931 St Leger.

9. A running track and a football club, the horse, which was probably not named after either of them, won the French Derby in 1977 and then finished third in the Arc.

10. A top athlete in his own right, this winner of the 1965 Scottish Grand National eventually went on to lend his name to a boot.

'THE SPORT OF KINGS'...

Each horse has 'King' in its name.

1. This colt was good enough to beat Giant's Causeway in the 2,000 Guineas of 2000.

2. This horse gave Willie Carson and John Gosden a Stewards' Cup victory at Goodwood in 1993.

3. This Francois Boutin-trained horse, ridden by Cash Asmussen, danced its way to the front in Ascot's St James's Palace Stakes in 1993.

4. Pat Eddery got this one home for Vincent O'Brien in the 1981 Sussex Stakes.

5. Which Khalid Abdullah horse, trained by John Gosden and ridden by James Doyle, won Ascot's St James's Palace Stakes in 2014?

6. This King brought home the gold for trainer Derrick Candy and lightweight jockey Des Cullen in the 1971 Cambridgeshire.

7. This colt, with Mick Kinane up, gave Aidan O'Brien his first 2,000 Guineas success in 1998.

8. The last two-year-old to win the Nunthorpe Stakes did it for John Best, Jimmy Quinn and owner John Mayne in 2007.

9. This horse, trained by Paul Nicholls, provided Tony McCoy with his solitary success in the Scottish Grand National, in 1997.

10. Trendy London thoroughfare lands the 2000 running of the Hennessy Gold Cup for Nigel Twiston-Davies and jockey Jamie Goldstein.

QUIZ No 64

...'AND QUEENS.'

Each of these horses has 'Queen' in its name.

1. Perhaps this horse had the heart of a lion when it won the Wokingham at Ascot in 1980 for Paul Cole and Geoff Baxter.

2. This horse won the 1963 running of the Lockinge Stakes at Newbury for trainer Atty Corbett, jockey Scobie Breasley and owner Lord Carnarvon.

3. Trained by David Elsworth and ridden by Silvestre de Sousa, this horse sprang a big surprise at odds of 50-1 when it won the Juddmonte International at York in 2015.

4. Something of a specialist when the Scottish Grand National was run at Bogside, with three wins, it jointly holds the record for victories in the race. Trained by Herbert Clarkson, it won in 1953, 1954 and 1956.

5. Sometimes called the best filly not to win a Classic, Mick Channon's charge, after an undefeated two-year-old career that saw her win the Queen Mary, Lowther and Cheveley Park Stakes in 2001, was retired before the next year's 1,000 Guineas.

6. Ryan Moore and Aidan O'Brien's 2012 winner of the 1,000 Guineas sounds like a returning sovereign.

7. Whether it is celebrated naturally in April or officially in June, it certainly won the Northumberland Plate of 1891. What do you mean you can't remember it!

8. This odds-on winner of the 1959 Cheveley Park Stakes for trainer Jack Waugh and jockey Eph Smith was definitely not on Oscar Wilde's Christmas card list!

9. Titania by another name, this filly won the July Cup in 1890.

10. The arrival of this ancient monarch was orchestrated by Handel and she also won the Hunt Cup at Royal Ascot in 1952 for Atty Persse and Frank Barlow.

'STRANGELY ENOUGH.' PART ONE.

1. In 2009 a horse ridden by Tony McCoy and trained by Carl Llewellyn, named after a sponsor and producer of an alcoholic drink, won a race originally sponsored and still widely known by the name of another producer of an alcoholic drink. What was the name of the horse?

2. If you took a train journey from the winner of the 1972 1,000 Guineas to the winner of the 2010 Mill Reef Stakes which two cities would be involved?

3. Which two post-war England international goalkeepers have won the Grand National?

4. On August 23, 2011, at Leicester, the winning horse, jockey and trainer of one of the races on the card all carried the same name. What was it?

5. Perhaps it was the Mafia that ensured no-one ever heard which Martin Pipe-trained, Adrian Maguire-ridden horse won the 1991 Irish Grand National!

6. Which current Hungerford-based trainer sounds like an underground station on the Jubilee Line?

7. Between 1980 and 2011 the Champion Hurdle was won by five winged creatures (four horses and a jockey). Which ones?

8. Dragon Fly was the 100-9 winner of the 1955 Newbury Autumn Cup. A horse of the same name won a fictitious race at Devon and Exeter in the mid-1970s at 14-1. Who had £5 on it but never saw a penny of his winnings?

9. The winner of Ascot's Long Walk Hurdle in 1990 is also present in a former Chelsea striker, one half of a rock group, an American outlaw, a former World Heavyweight Champion, a four-time Major-winning golfer, and the location of the Valley, home of Charlton Athletic FC. What was the horse's name?

10. Which jockey has won successive Stewards' Cups in different centuries?

....

'STRANGELY ENOUGH.' PART TWO.

1. In the memorable Eclipse Stakes of 2000, Giant's Causeway and Kalanisi were first and second. What was the combined age of their riders, George Duffield and Pat Eddery?

2. When Labour politician Robin Cook was the castaway on Desert Island Discs which book did he choose?

3. Which eventual winner of the Cheltenham Gold Cup was twice beaten by a short head in earlier runnings of the race?

4. Between 1971 and 1975 the Champion Hurdle winner was trained five years in a row by a 'Fred.' Who were the two men involved?

5. Which Derby winner, this century, had 230 owners?

6. After the furore and subsequent trial concerning the Chester Cup win of Top Cees in 1995, what was the appropriate name of the horse that won the race the year after Top Cees had won it for a second time?

7. What was unique about Latrobe's victory in the 2018 Irish Derby?

8. Put one letter in front of the jockey who won the 1994 Champion Hurdle on Flakey Dove and you produce the jockey aboard Hardy Eustace in his two wins in the race of 2004 and 2005. Who are the two jockeys?

9. The winner of Chester's Dee Stakes in 1989, trained by Barry Hills and ridden by his son Michael, could be either someone who perspires readily or a jersey you didn't have to pay for! What was it called?

10. The winning jockeys' surnames in Kempton's King George VI Chase for seven years in a row between 2006 and 2012 began with the same letter. Who were the two jockeys involved?

'THREES.' PART ONE – HORSES.

Each of these horses has won the same race three years running.

1. Which horse, trained by Vincent O'Brien and ridden by Aubrey Brabazon, won successive Cheltenham Gold Cups between 1948 and 1950?

2. Colin Davies-trained and Jimmy Uttley-ridden, which horse landed the Champion Hurdle three times from 1968 to 1970?

3. Which chestnut, trained by Jeremy Tree, took three consecutive William Hill Sprint Championships (Nunthorpes) at York between 1980 and 1982?

4. Abandonment of the meeting due to foot and mouth disease in 2001 prevented which horse from trying for a record four Champion Hurdles in a row?

5. From 1964 to 1966 the Cheltenham Gold Cup was synonymous with one horse. You know his name!

6. In the early years of the century which horse provided Henrietta Knight and Jim Culloty with three consecutive years of Gold Cup wins?

7. Which horse did Nick Williams saddle to dominate Ascot's Long Walk Hurdle from 2012 to 2014?

8. Which horse gave Vincent O'Brien three successive Champion Hurdle victories?

9. Trained by Nicky Henderson and ridden by Steve Smith Eccles, which horse landed three Champion Hurdles between 1985 and 1987?

10. Which horse, trained on one occasion by Monica Dickinson and on two occasions by Michael Dickinson and ridden by Robert Earnshaw, won the Queen Mother Champion Chase three times between 1983 and 1985?

QUIZ No 68

'THREES.' PART TWO – JOCKEYS.

Each of these jockeys has won the same race three years running.

1. Which jockey won three consecutive Benson & Hedges Gold Cups at York in the 1980s aboard Beldale Flutter, Assert and Caerleon?

2. Who is the only jockey in the 20th century to win three successive Doncaster St Legers, in 1970, 1971 and 1972?

3. Fleet Wahine, Attica Meli and Mysterious were the three horses involved in which jockey's Yorkshire Oaks treble between 1971 and 1973?

4. Who is the only jockey in the approximately 240 years of the race to win the Derby three times in a row?

5. Royal Ascot's Coventry Stakes was won three times in succession between 1961 and 1963 by Xerxes, Crocket and Showdown. Which five-time champion jockey partnered all three?

6. Singapore, Foxhunter and Colorado Kid provided which legendary jockey with three Doncaster Cups between 1931 and 1933?

7. Which Australian jockey landed Goodwood's Richmond Stakes three times between 1963 and 1965 on Gentle Art, Ragtime and Sky Gipsy?

8. Between 1959 and 1961 Cutter, Aggressor and High Perch were successive winners of Newbury's John Porter Stakes. They were all ridden by the same jockey, who later went to work for the BBC. Who was he?

9. Which jockey, who was sadly killed on the same track later in the decade, won Ascot's Queen Mary Stakes three years in a row between 1951 and 1953 on Primavera, Devon Vintage and Sybil's Niece?

10. Which jockey completed a treble in the 1,000 Guineas during the First World War on Vaucluse, Canyon and Diadem?

'THREES.' PART THREE – TRAINERS.

Each of these trainers has won the same race three times running.

1. Which trainer was successful three times in a row in the Ascot Gold Cup in the 1990s? The horses involved were Indian Queen and Drum Taps, twice.

2. Which trainer won the Gimcrack Stakes at York three times consecutively between 1956 and 1958 with Eudaemon, Pheidippides and Be Careful?

3. Which French trainer produced Sagaro to dominate the Ascot Gold Cup with wins in 1975, 1976 and 1977?

4. Which trainer sent out Sir Ken to take the Champion Hurdle in 1952, 1953 and 1954?

5. Between 1969 and 1971 High Line won the Jockey Club Cup at Newmarket three times. He was ridden on each occasion by Joe Mercer. Who trained the horse?

6. From 1974 to 1976, with Colebridge and Brown Lad, twice, which trainer won the Irish Grand National three times?

7. Which Irish trainer plundered both Sandown's National Stakes and Doncaster's Champagne Stakes three times in a row in the 1960s?

8. The trainer of 19 Classic winners, he also saddled the winners of three consecutive Northumberland Plates between 1954 and 1956.

9. Which trainer landed three Goodwood Cups in a row between 1964 and 1966, the last two for the Queen?

10. Between 1975 and 1977 who trained the winner of the Irish St Leger three times?

TOP JOCKEYS – FLAT. FRANKIE DETTORI.

1. Of Frankie Dettori's 18 British Classic wins, only one was on a horse with three words in its name. Which one?

2. Seventeen of them were won at Newmarket, Epsom and Doncaster. On which course did he win the other one?

3. Frankie Dettori's most recent of three victories in the Dubai World Cup came in 2006 for Godolphin. On which horse?

4. Dettori's first British Classic win in 1994 came in that year's Oaks at Epsom for trainer Hilal Ibrahim. The filly concerned then entered the Irish Derby and gave Frankie his only winner in that race. Who was she?

5. Which race has Dettori won three times with Polytain in 1992, Shamardal in 2005 and Lawman in 2007?

6. Of Frankie's 'Magnificent Seven' at Ascot in September 1996, Saeed Bin Suroor trained four and Sir Michael Stoute and John Gosden one each. The other horse was Lochangel. Who trained it?

7. Among his celebrations that day, Dettori decided to buy the horse he was on when he won his seventh race. What was it called?

8. Frankie has won one British Classic for trainer Hugo Palmer. What was the horse's name and the race he won?

9. Which of the five British Classics did Frankie Dettori fail to win in the 20th century?

10. Which race has Dettori won on two occasions, firstly with West Wind in 2007 and most recently with Star Of Seville in 2015?

TOP JOCKEYS – FLAT. KIEREN FALLON.

1. Which of the five British Classics did Kieren Fallon fail to win?

2. Fallon sustained a serious injury in a race in 2000 that left him on the sidelines for several months and threatened his career. On which racecourse did it occur?

3. Fallon won the Ebor Handicap for the only time in 1998, when the Henry Cecil-trained 9-2 favourite did the business. What was it called?

4. Fallon won back-to-back Queen Alexandra Stakes at Royal Ascot in 2002 and 2003 on a Sir Michael Stoute-trained stayer with a nice turn of foot. What was its name?

5. Fallon won his second Cesarewitch in 2012 for trainer Brian Meehan on a horse that had already won the race two years before. What was it called?

6. A lovely filly, under Fallon she won a Nassau Stakes, two Yorkshire Oaks and the Breeders' Cup Filly & Mare Turf in the years 2002 and 2003 for trainer Sir Michael Stoute. Who was she?

7. Kieren rode Yeats in one of his four history-making wins in the Ascot Gold Cup but he also won the 2003 running of the race when which Paul Cole-trained horse prevailed?

8. On which smart sprinter did Kieren Fallon land the Haydock Sprint Cup of 2012 for trainer James Fanshawe?

9. Fallon's 16 British Classic wins were dominated by three trainers; Henry Cecil, Sir Michael Stoute and Aidan O'Brien trained 14 of the 16. Two other trainers provided one winner each to complete Fallon's impressive tally. Who are they?

10. Kieren's sole win in the Lincoln Handicap came in 1993 aboard which horse of Lynda Ramsden's?

TOP JOCKEYS – FLAT. RYAN MOORE.

1. As of 2018 Ryan Moore had ridden eight British Classic winners for Aidan O'Brien. Who is the only other Irish trainer he has won a British Classic for?

2. Which horse did Ryan Moore complete a Derby and Arc double on for trainer Sir Michael Stoute in 2010?

3. In 2014 Ryan Moore won the Cox Plate for Aidan O'Brien in one Australian city with a horse named for another Australian city. What was it called?

4. Ryan won the Racing Post Trophy on this horse in 2017 but frustratingly didn't ride it when it duly won the next year's 2,000 Guineas. What was its name?

5. Ryan Moore's only winner of the French Derby was on The Grey Gatsby in 2014. Who trained it?

6. Early in his riding career, in 2002, Moore won the Cesarewitch at Newmarket aboard Miss Fara for which jumps trainer?

7. Ryan Moore won the Breeders' Cup Juvenile Turf on this horse in 2017 and then, in 2018, took the UAE Derby on the same horse. What was it called?

8. As of 2018, Ryan Moore has won two King Georges at Ascot with the Sir Michael Stoute-trained Conduit in 2009 and the Aidan O'Brien-trained Highland Reel in 2016. They were both market leaders and went off at the same price. What was it?

9. On a great two days at Epsom in June 2010 Ryan went from no Classic victories to two when he won the Oaks and the Derby. Which filly of Ed Dunlop's set the ball rolling for him on the Friday by landing the Oaks?

10. Which horse who finished third in the 2011 Derby had earlier won the Dante Stakes at York for the Queen with Ryan Moore up?

TOP JOCKEYS – FLAT. LESTER PIGGOTT.

1. What links the following four horses in Lester's career as a jockey? Gay Time, Meadow Court, Ribocco and Cavo Doro.

2. Of Lester's nine Derby winners only Nijinsky and The Minstrel were sired by the same horse. Which horse?

3. When Lester won the Arc in 1977 and 1978 on the same horse this feat was not repeated for 40 years. What was the name of Lester's double Arc winner?

4. Crepello, Sir Ivor and Nijinsky all won the 2,000 Guineas with Piggott aboard before going on to win the Derby with him as well. Which were the only two horses he won the 2,000 Guineas on that didn't go on to win the Derby?

5. Lester won a Classic for three trainers whose names begin with a 'W'. Who are the three trainers?

6. What happened seven days before Lester's 1981 1,000 Guineas triumph at Newmarket on Fairy Footsteps?

7. Between 1953 and 1959 Lester competed in 54 hurdle races, winning 20 of them. Fourteen of these wins were for one trainer, who?

8. On August 18, 1948, the 12-year-old Lester won on a horse called The Chase in the Wigan Lane Selling Handicap over a mile to record his first success on the Flat. At which racecourse did this happen?

9. Which British golf course did Lester ride into sixth place in the 1959 Epsom Derby?

10. What two words is Piggott allegedly said to have whispered in Vincent O'Brien's ear after the latter's horse, 2,000 Guineas winner El Gran Senor, had been beaten in a photo for the 1984 Derby under Pat Eddery?

TOP JOCKEYS – FLAT. SIR GORDON RICHARDS.

1. How many jockeys' titles did Gordon Richards win?

2. He may well have added one more to the tally had he not lost most of the 1926 season to which illness?

3. In 1921 he had his first ride at a track that no longer exists but its name lives on as an annual race on the Flat. Where was it?

4. Gordon's first Royal Ascot winner was in the 1925 running of the Queen Anne Stakes when his horse was the name of a north-east football club. What was it called?

5. From 1932 until 1951 Gordon Richards dominated a particular Royal Ascot race for two-year-olds, winning it nine times and, at one point, recording four wins from five starts. What was the race?

6. On which racecourse in 1933 did Gordon Richards ride 11 of the 12 winners over the two-day meeting?

7. Which filly constituted the only horse he won two Classics with, the 1942 1,000 Guineas and Oaks? There is now a race named after her at Newmarket.

8. Gordon Richards won the 1947 2,000 Guineas by the biggest margin since 1900 on a legendary horse. It wasn't until Frankel came along in the next century that such a performance was seen in the race again. What was the horse called?

9. When Gordon was finally successful in his 28th attempt in the Derby on the Norman Bertie-trained Pinza in 1953 who was the owner of the horse?

10. As a trainer, Gordon had a great miler who carried all before it as a three-year-old in 1967, winning the St James's Palace Stakes, Sussex Stakes and Champion Stakes. Who was it?

TOP JOCKEYS – JUMPS. JOHN FRANCOME.

1. Which horse did John Francome partner to victory in the Hennessy Gold Cup, King George VI Chase and Welsh Grand National?

2. John drew a blank in the Aintree, Midland and Irish Nationals, but won a Scottish Grand National in 1980 when Narvik was successful. Who trained Narvik?

3. With seven jockeys' titles to his name, John Francome is third on the list of jumps jockeys. Obviously, Tony McCoy heads the list but who is in second place with eight championships?

4. John Francome won the Tingle Creek Chase at Sandown in successive years in 1981 and 1982 on which Fred Winter-trained horse?

5. On which previous Champion Hurdle winner did John Francome take Ascot's Long Walk Hurdle in 1975?

6. On which horse, trained by Fred Winter, did John Francome win the 1983 Hennessy Gold Cup at Newbury?

7. John Francome took the first running of the Cleeve Hurdle at Cheltenham in 1983 on another Fred Winter-trained horse. What was it called?

8. In 1981 John Francome recorded his only Champion Hurdle success when which Peter Easterby-trained horse won the race for a second time?

9. Which horse, trained by Michael Dickinson, was a King George VI Chase winner at Kempton for John Francome in 1982, one of three wins the horse achieved in that particular race?

10. The postponement through snow of the Cheltenham Gold Cup in 1978 led to the race being run in April under conditions that suited John Francome's mount. It turned out to be the one and only time that both trainer Fred Winter and jockey John Francome won the race. An appreciative crowd cheered home which horse?

QUIZ No 76

TOP JOCKEYS – JUMPS. RICHARD JOHNSON.

1. Which horse of Philip Hobbs did Richard Johnson have a great year with at Cheltenham in 2010, taking the Supreme Novices' Hurdle, the Greatwood Hurdle and finishing off with the Stan James International Hurdle?

2. With which horse, trained by Philip Hobbs, did Richard Johnson win the Queen Mother Champion Chase at Cheltenham in 2002?

3. It wasn't all plain sailing in the Queen Mother Champion Chase when Richard Johnson was partnering a Philip Hobbs horse. In the 2012 race, won by Finian's Rainbow, which horse deposited him head first into the crowd in front of the stands, where he luckily sustained no serious injury?

4. Richard Johnson twice won the race most of us still call the Whitbread, firstly in 2006 when it was called the Betfred Gold Cup and, secondly, in 2008, by which time it had become the bet365 Gold Cup. Which were the two winning horses?

5. The answer I would give if asked whether Richard Johnson will eventually overhaul Tony McCoy's total of winners was also the name of the horse that brought up Johnson's 2000th winner at Newbury in 2009. What was it called?

6. After winning the 2002 County Hurdle on Terry Warner's grey for Philip Hobbs, Richard Johnson landed his, to date, only Champion Hurdle success on the same horse in the following year. Name the horse.

7. Who trained Looks Like Trouble when he became Richard Johnson's first Cheltenham Gold Cup winner in 2000?

8. Richard Johnson's first winner was on a horse called Rusty Bridge at his local course in April 1994. Which course?

9. On which Shropshire course did Richard Johnson record his 3000th winner aboard St Saviour in 2016?

10. Richard Johnson, to date, has won Ascot's Long Walk Hurdle four times, twice with Reve De Sivola for Nick Williams and, in the last century, on Anzum for Alan King. Between these, in 2006, he won it on a horse trained by Henry Daly. What was it called?

TOP JOCKEYS – JUMPS. SIR ANTHONY McCOY.

1. When the Whitbread Gold Cup upset traditionalists and became the 'At The Races' Gold Cup in 2002, Tony McCoy registered the first of his two wins in the race on a horse trained by Martin Pipe whose name summed up AP's attitude to the many setbacks with injuries that he suffered. What was the horse called?

2. When AP won the William Hill Trophy at the 2009 Cheltenham Festival many considered it his greatest ever ride. On which horse?

3. On which horse did AP win his only Queen Mother Champion Chase at Cheltenham in the year 2000?

4. In 2002 Tony McCoy won a charity Flat race for jump jockeys at which southern track?

5. In a strange race at Southwell on January 23, 2002, all seven runners fell. However, AP McCoy got back on board the favourite to land the spoils. Which horse did he win on?

6. Which horse have both Tony McCoy and Ruby Walsh ridden to victory in the Irish Champion Hurdle?

7. AP finally got to win the Grand National in 2010, but it had looked likely in 2005 when he was taken out at Becher's on the second circuit. Who was the unlucky horse?

8. Tony McCoy's first winner was on a horse called Legal Steps on March 26, 1992 at the age of 17 at Thurles, in Ireland. Which trainer was he riding for?

9. Until retiring in April 2015, McCoy had dominated the jump jockeys' championship. How many consecutive years did he win the title?

10. Which horse of Martin Pipe's did AP twice finish third on in the Grand Nationals of 2001 and 2002?

TOP JOCKEYS – JUMPS. RUBY WALSH.

1. Ruby Walsh is closely associated with Hurricane Fly's two Champion Hurdle victories at Cheltenham but which event did he win four years in a row on the same horse?

2. He is also closely linked to Kauto Star, on whom he won five King George VI Chases at Kempton, the first four consecutively. In those four races only one horse finished in the frame behind Kauto Star more than once. Who was he?

3. Who trained Papillon, Ruby's first Grand National winner, in 2000?

4. Hedgehunter, the horse that provided Ruby Walsh with his only other Grand National winner in 2005, came close to winning the Cheltenham Gold Cup as well in the following season when he finished second in the race to which horse?

5. Ruby Walsh won the Irish Grand National in 2005 on a horse who, frustratingly for him, went on to win the Aintree Grand National the next year at Ruby's expense, as he finished second on Hedgehunter. Who was the horse?

6. It looked like business as usual for Ruby Walsh when he won the opener at the Cheltenham Festival of 2019 for trainer Willie Mullins. However, unlike previous years, his victory in the Supreme Novices' Hurdle turned out to be his sole festival success. What was the winning horse's name?

7. Ruby Walsh had never won the Stayers' Hurdle at Cheltenham when, like London buses, four came along in a row in the shape of Big Buck's. He has, however, won the race since, being successful on which Willie Mullins-trained horse in 2017?

8. Ruby Walsh won the Punchestown Champion Stayers Hurdle on five occasions, four of them for trainer Willie Mullins. In the other one, in 2006, who trained the winner and what was it called?

9. Besides his epic win for trainer Paul Nicholls aboard Denman in the 2009 Hennessy Gold Cup at Newbury, Ruby Walsh also won the race for the same trainer in 2003; on which horse?

10. Ruby Walsh won Wetherby's Charlie Hall Chase just once, on which Paul Nicholls-trained horse in 2012?

TOP TRAINERS – FLAT. SIR HENRY CECIL.

1. In which country was Henry Cecil born?

2. Which 13-time Classic-winning trainer was Henry Cecil's stepfather?

3. In his overall total of 25 British Classics, which one did he win the least?

4. Henry Cecil's first winner as a trainer was with a horse called Celestial Cloud in 1969 on which Yorkshire track?

5. Henry Cecil's first Classic winner was not in England but came with Cloonagh in the Irish 1,000 Guineas of 1973. The jockey on board never won a British Classic for Cecil but was an Epsom Derby winner in his own right. Who was he?

6. With which Sheikh Mohammed colt, in 1989, did Henry Cecil achieve his sole victory in the French Derby?

7. With Midday, which race did Henry Cecil win three years in a row between 2009 and 2011?

8. Henry Cecil won his first Derby with Slip Anchor in 1985. His sire had also been a Derby winner. Who was he?

9. Which jockey won both fillies' Classics on horses trained by Henry Cecil but didn't win any other Classics for him?

10. Of the five jockeys who each recorded one British Classic success on Henry Cecil's horses, two of them have surnames that begin with the same letter. Who are they?

....

TOP TRAINERS – FLAT. JOHN GOSDEN.

1. Which two legendary trainers did John Gosden work for before going to work in America?

2. Gosden's big breakthrough came in 1983 when he trained the winner of the prestigious Santa Anita Handicap in front of an 85,000 crowd. Janet Leigh probably didn't back it! Name the horse.

3. Six jockeys have ridden a British Classic winner trained by John Gosden. The surnames of two of them begin with the same letter. Which two?

4. In 1984 John Gosden trained a filly to win the inaugural running of the Breeders' Cup Mile, owned by Robert Sangster and ridden by Fernando Toro. Who was she?

5. Which Wim Wenders film won York's Dante Stakes for Frankie Dettori and John Gosden in 2016?

6. Which speedster took both the July Cup and the Nunthorpe for John Gosden, Richard Hughes and Khalid Abdullah in 2003?

7. William Buick's first major win as a jockey for John Gosden came in the 2010 running of the Dubai Sheema Classic. On which horse?

8. This top-class stayer, trained by John Gosden, played second fiddle to no-one between 2017 and 2019 when he was successful on more than one occasion in both the Ascot Gold Cup and the Goodwood Cup. Who is he?

9. Which Gosden-trained horse is fondly remembered for a number of great battles with Henrythenavigator and for nailing the Breeders' Cup Classic in 2008 under Frankie Dettori at Santa Anita?

10. Among the top races this filly won between 2012 and 2014 were the Musidora Stakes and Nassau Stakes, the Yorkshire Oaks, Irish Champion Stakes and Ascot's Prince of Wales Stakes. She certainly, like Bach, struck the right note most of the time. What was her name?

TOP TRAINERS – FLAT. AIDAN O'BRIEN.

1. Why was Camelot's Derby win in 2012 unique in the history of the race?

2. Which filly completed the Oaks treble for O'Brien in 2006 by winning the Epsom, Yorkshire and Irish versions of the race?

3. Which two jockeys have both won the St Leger for Aidan O'Brien but have won no other Classics for him?

4. In 2008, Aidan O'Brien achieved something in Irish racing that had last happened 73 years before. What was it?

5. Aidan O'Brien trained a John Lennon song to win the 2001 Irish 1,000 Guineas and, two years later, trained a Paul McCartney song to win the same race. Who were the two horses?

6. In 2005, Aidan O'Brien delivered, with assistance from Kieren Fallon, the British Guineas' double. Which two horses were involved?

7. Which jockey has won the Oaks on an Aidan O'Brien-trained horse, but hasn't won any other British Classics for him?

8. Which is the only horse trained by Aidan O'Brien to win both the Ascot Gold Cup and St Leger?

9. In 2017 Aidan O'Brien broke the world record for training Group 1 winners in a calendar year. How many?

10. Which horse, trained by Aidan O'Brien, won seven Group 1 races in a row between October 2001 and September 2002?

TOP TRAINERS – FLAT. VINCENT O'BRIEN.

1. Vincent O'Brien won 16 British Classics as a trainer. Did Lester Piggott ride more or less than half of them?

2. This colt later went on to become the greatest European sire of his era. In his racing days he won the 1984 Irish 2,000 Guineas, the Eclipse Stakes and the Irish Champion Stakes. Who was he?

3. The 1,000 Guineas was Vincent O'Brien's least successful Classic. He won it just once, in 1966, with Glad Rags. Who rode her?

4. Which decade brought the most Epsom Derby winners for Vincent O'Brien, the 1960s, 1970s or 1980s?

5. Who was the only jockey to ride the winner of the same Classic two years in a row for Vincent O'Brien?

6. Which well-known race did he win just once, with Gladness, ridden by Lester Piggott in 1958?

7. Vincent O'Brien trained one French Derby winner, ridden by Pat Eddery in 1983. What was the horse called?

8. Who rode Nijinsky when he won the Irish Derby in 1970?

9. Which sprinter, trained by O'Brien and ridden by Piggott, won the Haydock Sprint Cup in 1972 and followed up the next year with Ascot's King's Stand Stakes?

10. Which race did Vincent O'Brien win 15 times between 1967 and 1992?

TOP TRAINERS – FLAT. SIR MICHAEL STOUTE.

1. Sir Michael Stoute holds a 20th century record for winning at least one British Classic in how many successive seasons?

2. The last letter in the alphabet appears twice in the name of the horse Stoute trained to land both the Sussex Stakes and the Queen Elizabeth II Stakes under Walter Swinburn in 1989. What was it called?

3. In the second running of the Dubai World Cup in 1997 Sir Michael Stoute and jockey Jerry Bailey took the prize with which horse of Sheikh Mohammed's?

4. Which horse gave Sir Michael Stoute his only King's Stand victory at Royal Ascot in 1981?

5. Which Group 1 race has Sir Michael Stoute won eight times, beginning with Scottish Reel in 1986 for owners Cheveley Park Stud?

6. Who has won the most British Classics riding horses trained by Sir Michael Stoute; Walter Swinburn or Kieren Fallon?

7. In 2009 Sir Michael Stoute produced something of a rarity by training Conduit, Tartan Bearer and Ask to be the first three past the post in which race?

8. After showing promise as a two-year-old by winning the 1986 Dewhurst Stakes this horse finished ninth in Reference Point's Derby before being sent sprinting. He took to it very well, winning the July Cup, Nunthorpe Stakes and Haydock Sprint Cup that same year for Sheikh Mohammed. Who was he?

9. With which horse did Sir Michael Stoute achieve the considerable feat in 2008 and 2009 of winning back-to-back Breeders' Cup Turfs in America?

10. Greville Starkey rode the filly who gave Sir Michael Stoute his first British Classic by winning the Oaks in 1978. What was her name?

TOP TRAINERS – FLAT. SAEED BIN SUROOR.

1. Who is the only Australian jockey to ride the winner of a Classic trained by Saeed Bin Suroor?

2. This Saeed Bin Suroor-trained colt finished second in the 2000 Derby before going on to win the following year's Arc. Who was he?

3. Which was the only horse trained by Saeed Bin Suroor to win both the Ascot Gold Cup and the St Leger?

4. With which filly did Saeed Bin Suroor complete a 1,000 Guineas and Oaks double in 2002?

5. This Godolphin colt won the 2005 running of the Irish 2,000 Guineas and finished third in Motivator's Derby in the same year. However, his racing career has been overshadowed by his enormous success as a stallion. Who is he?

6. In the late 1990s Saeed Bin Suroor managed the difficult feat of winning successive King Georges at Ascot with the same horse. Which one?

7. This lovely grey won the 1998 Eclipse Stakes at Sandown, then went to America to take the Man O'War Stakes at Belmont Park before returning to win the Coronation Cup and King George in 1999, before finishing off the year by going back to the States in November to win the Breeders' Cup Turf. Who was he?

8. Probably the most appropriately named horse ever to win a race when he took the 2000 running of the Dubai World Cup at Meydan under Frankie Dettori.

9. Named after a former cricketer who captained Pakistan, this colt, who never contested a Group 1 event, nevertheless was so impressive in demolishing the opposition in both the Diomed Stakes and the Queen Anne Stakes for Saeed Bin Suroor in 1998 that he is still remembered today. He also sired a Classic winner in Snow Fairy. Who was he?

10. One of Godolphin's stars, this colt was a high achiever who, in 2000, won both the Hong Kong Cup and the Man O'War Stakes. Then, in 2001, he took the Irish Champion Stakes and Breeders' Cup Turf. Who was he?

TOP TRAINERS – JUMPS. NICKY HENDERSON.

1. Named after his father, the Johnny Henderson Grand Annual Chase at the Cheltenham Festival is a race that Nicky Henderson always likes to have a runner in. It didn't take him long to win it, when Andrew Tinkler rode which horse to victory in 2006?

2. Nicky Henderson learnt his craft as assistant to which legendary trainer from 1974 to 1978?

3. After a Triumph Hurdle success for Nicky Henderson in 2009, which horse then went on to finish third in the following year's Champion Hurdle?

4. Nicky Henderson won Kempton's King George VI Chase in 2017 with which horse?

5. When Binocular won the 2010 Champion Hurdle it constituted Nicky Henderson's fifth win in the race. Which trainer's record did it equal?

6. Nicky Henderson won his father's race for a second time at the Cheltenham Festival in 2012 with which horse, owned by JP McManus and ridden by Paul Carberry?

7. Nicky Henderson won the Queen Mother Champion Chase for the first time in 1992 with Remittance Man. Who rode him?

8. That superb horse Sprinter Sacre won the Queen Mother Champion Chase in 2013 in astonishing fashion and bounced back from heart problems to take it again three years later. A different jockey rode him each time. Which two men were involved?

9. In the 2015 edition of the Triumph Hurdle Nicky Henderson had great success in managing to train the first three horses home, with a neck between the winner and the runner-up at the line. They were ridden by Barry Geraghty and Daryl Jacob. Who was first and second?

10. Nicky Henderson has never won the Grand National but he came very close when his first ever runner in the race, in 1979, came second behind Rubstic, beaten one and a half lengths. What was his runner called?

TOP TRAINERS – JUMPS. 'A CHIP OFF THE OLD BLOCK' – THE McCAINS.

1. 'Ginger' McCain will be forever associated with Red Rum but who owned the horse?

2. The battle between Red Rum and Crisp is arguably the finest moment in Grand National history but on that day a future Grand National winner with two Cheltenham Gold Cups under his belt was left trailing 25 lengths behind the pair, in third place. Who was he?

3. Red Rum carried 10st 5lb to victory when he beat Crisp in 1973. How much did he carry when he won the National again the following year?

4. Which three jockeys have won the Grand National on a horse trained by 'Ginger' McCain?

5. Ginger's fourth National win came in 2004 with Amberleigh House, a mere 27 years after Rummy's last success. To the present day he was the oldest horse to win the race. How old was he?

6. Which horse provided Donald McCain jnr with a winner in the 2010 Neptune Novices' Hurdle at the Cheltenham Festival?

7. Donald McCain jnr was a popular winner of the Grand National with the Trevor Hemmings-owned Ballabriggs in 2011. Who rode it?

8. Which race did Donald McCain jnr win in successive years in 2010 and 2011 with Peddler's Cross and Overturn?

9. He was successful in training the winner of the Supreme Novices' Hurdle at Cheltenham in 2012 with which horse?

10. With which horse of Donald McCain jnr's did Timmy Murphy win the Charlie Hall Chase at Wetherby in 2011?

TOP TRAINERS – JUMPS. WILLIE MULLINS.

1. As of 2019, Willie Mullins has won only one Grand National, which he won in 2005 with which horse?

2. Of his nine winners of the Champion Bumper at the Cheltenham Festival just one went on to win Kempton's King George VI Chase. It happened to the 1997 bumper winner and he won the 2001 King George VI Chase. Who was he?

3. Willie Mullins has landed Sandown's Tingle Creek Chase just once, in 2016, with which horse?

4. Willie Mullins set a new record for wins at the Cheltenham Festival with eight in 2015. The record lasted only three years before it was equalled by which trainer?

5. Willie Mullins has a truly remarkable record in the David Nicholson Mares' Hurdle. Up to now he has won the race in nine of the last 11 years. Which mare won six of those nine consecutively?

6. When Annie Power fell at the last in the 2015 Mares' Hurdle it foiled a Ruby Walsh and Willie Mullins four-timer that allegedly saved bookmakers between £40 million and £100 million. It didn't worry Mullins over much because it handed the race to another of his contenders, ridden by Paul Townend. What was the winning mare called?

7. Willie Mullins has farmed the Arkle Chase at Cheltenham, winning it in 2015, 2016, 2018 and 2019. He would have been successful in 2014 as well but his highly fancied horse was touched off on the line by David Pipe's 33-1 shot, Western Warhorse. What was the name of the beaten Mullins horse?

8. In the Champion Bumper at Cheltenham this century, the riding duties in five of their six wins have been split between the Mullins and Walsh families, featuring Ruby and Katie Walsh and Patrick Mullins. This pattern was broken in Joe Cullen's win in 2000. Who rode that one?

9. In 2015 Willie Mullins achieved something that hadn't been done before when he trained the first three home in the Champion Hurdle. Faugheen won the race and Hurricane Fly was third. What was second at 20-1?

10. Willie Mullins had his first winner as a trainer at the Cheltenham Festival in 1995 when which horse prevailed in the Supreme Novices' Hurdle?

TOP TRAINERS – JUMPS. PAUL NICHOLLS.

1. Who is the only jockey to win the Cheltenham Gold Cup on a Paul Nicholls-trained horse in the last century?

2. Which horse won back-to-back Queen Mother Champion Chases at the Cheltenham Festival for Paul Nicholls in 2008 and 2009?

3. In 2012 Rock On Ruby provided Paul Nicholls with his only Champion Hurdle win, under which jockey?

4. Which top race did Paul Nicholls win seven times in nine years between 2006 and 2014?

5. Paul Nicholls has been successful twice in the Triumph Hurdle, in 2008 and 2011. Which two horses did he win with?

6. In both 2007 and 2009, which horse twice carried 11st 12lb to victory around Newbury in the Hennessy Gold Cup for Paul Nicholls? Awesome stuff!

7. Which horse provided Paul Nicholls with his sole victory in the Grand National, at 33-1 in 2012?

8. Which Paul Nicholls-trained horse accomplished an unprecedented feat in capturing the World Hurdle at Cheltenham four times successively between 2009 and 2012?

9. Paul Nicholls won his 50th Grade 1 race in December 2008 when Master Minded and Tony McCoy won which prestigious chase?

10. Paul Nicholls trained his first winner, Olveston, in 1991. Why was this of special significance for him?

TOP TRAINERS – JUMPS. VINCENT O'BRIEN.

1. Which race did Vincent O'Brien win in 1952 with a horse called Alberoni?

2. Who was the only jockey besides Aubrey Brabazon to win both the Champion Hurdle and Cheltenham Gold Cup for Vincent O'Brien?

3. Before landing the 1954 Grand National for Vincent O'Brien, Royal Tan had finished second to Nickel Coin in the 1951 running of the race. Who rode him in 1951?

4. Has Vincent O'Brien ever trained the winner of the Scottish Grand National?

5. Vincent O'Brien achieved the seemingly impossible feat of training the winner of the Grand National three years running, with Early Mist, Royal Tan and Quare Times, in 1953, 1954 and 1955. Did these three horses ever run against each other in a Grand National?

6. Cottage Rake won three Cheltenham Gold Cups between 1948 and 1950 for Vincent O'Brien. In 1948 he also won another significant race in England. What was it?

7. The sum total of Cottage Rake's earnings for three Gold Cup wins in a row amounted to less than £8,000. True or false?

8. Vincent O'Brien's three successive Champion Hurdle wins have been matched by four other trainers. Who are they?

9. Which innovative method of transport did Vincent O'Brien use to get three of his horses to Cheltenham for the 1949 renewal?

10. Which horse, in both the 1954 and 1955 Grand Nationals, finished runner-up to Vincent O'Brien's winners?

TOP TRAINERS – JUMPS. THE PIPES ARE CALLING!

1. Which race was established at Cheltenham annually from 2009 in honour of Martin Pipe's training career?

2. Which horse, ridden by Paul Leach, put Martin Pipe firmly on the map by landing the 1981 Triumph Hurdle at 66-1?

3. Martin won the Grand National in 1994 with the Richard Dunwoody-ridden Miinnehoma. People who own racehorses are often thought to be comedians but this owner actually was one! What was his name?

4. Which two jockeys have ridden the winner of the Imperial Cup at Sandown for both Martin and David Pipe?

5. Which horse did David Pipe train for his father in 2007 that not only won the Imperial Cup but also took the Fred Winter Juvenile Handicap Hurdle at Cheltenham under Andrew Glassonbury to give father and son a large bonus payment?

6. Which much loved horse, unfortunate both with injuries and with being around at the same time as Moscow Flyer and Azertyuiop, won the Arkle Chase at Cheltenham in 2004 for AP McCoy and Martin Pipe?

7. The Grand National score between father and son is 'one all'. David won the race in 2008 with the Timmy Murphy-ridden Comply Or Die. Who owned the horse?

8. Father and son are also 'one all' where Cheltenham's Champion Bumper is concerned, Martin being successful in 2003 and David in 2015. Which two horses were involved?

9. Martin won the Hennessy Gold Cup three times. On two of those occasions, in 1988 and 2004, his two winning horses shared the same word in their names. What were the two horses called?

10. With which gutsy horse did David Pipe win Ascot's Long Walk Hurdle in 2007?

TRUE OR FALSE – THE FLAT.

1. Since the turn of the century, Frankie Dettori, William Buick and Ryan Moore are the only three jockeys to win back-to-back St Legers at Doncaster.

2. Paul Hanagan's only Classic win came on Taghrooda in the Oaks.

3. The St Leger was the only Classic that Walter Swinburn failed to win.

4. Pat Eddery, on Lomond in 1983 and El Gran Senor in 1984, was the first jockey since the War to win successive 2,000 Guineas.

5. Between 2013 and 2017 Aidan O'Brien trained the winner of the Chester Vase five times in a row.

6. Henry Cecil was the only trainer in the 1990s to win back-to-back 1,000 Guineas. He did it with Bosra Sham and Sleepytime.

7. When Frankie Dettori won successive Arcs on Enable in 2017 and 2018 this was the first time he had done this.

8. French-trained horses have won more than ten 1,000 Guineas since the War.

9. High Chaparral in 2002 was the first horse this century to win both the British and Irish Derbys.

10. Jockey Richard Hills won all the other four Classics but never won the Derby.

TRUE OF FALSE – THE JUMPS.

1. Noel Fehily's last Cheltenham Festival winner was a 50-1 shot for trainer Paul Nicholls aboard Eglantine Du Seuil.

2. Pat Taaffe's five wins as a jockey in the Queen Mother Champion Chase has still not been equalled.

3. Wayward Lad's three King George VI Chase wins in 1982, 1983 and 1985 were achieved with the help of three different jockeys.

4. Foinavon in 1967 and Mon Mome in 2009 were the only post-War Grand National winners to start at 100-1.

5. Since the War only three jockeys have won the Cheltenham Gold Cup three times in a row.

6. My Tent Or Yours, trained by Nicky Henderson and owned by JP McManus, was unlucky enough to be runner-up three times in the Champion Hurdle without ever winning it.

7. In the 21st century the King George VI Chase has been won six times in a row by horses beginning with the same letter.

8. Female jockeys enjoyed their most successful Cheltenham Festival in 2019 when Rachael Blackmore, Lizzie Kelly and Bryony Frost all won one race each.

9. In his career, jockey Mick Fitzgerald failed to win the Champion Hurdle.

10. Arkle's 1965 Cheltenham Gold Cup victory at 100-30 on was the shortest-priced winner of the race since World War Two.

UNLUCKY LOSERS – 'BORN UNDER A BAD SIGN.'

1. A horse trained by Peter Walwyn and ridden by Duncan Keith won the Ascot Gold Cup in 1971 and 1972 but doesn't appear as the winner in the record books, losing the first time to Random Shot due to an illegal substance and the second time to Erimo Hawk in the stewards' room. Who was the horse?

2. Which horse at Leopardstown in 2005 failed to win the Grade 1 Paddy Power Dial-A-Bet Chase because jockey Roger Loughran mistook the location of the winning post and celebrated prematurely? There were only five horses in the race and the other strange thing about it was that the odds-on Moscow Flyer could finish only fourth!

3. Which talented speed merchant, trained by Dick Hern and ridden by Willie Carson, was just getting the measure of Safely Kept inside the final furlong of the 1990 Breeders' Cup Sprint when he appeared to jump a shadow and lost the race?

4. In November 1969, Pinehurst Park, ridden by John Jenkins, easily won the Ascot Valley Gardens Handicap Hurdle, giving pleasure and financial reward to my old friend Dave Ashforth. Why did he have a different expression on his face seconds later?

5. Charlie Hills had a runner in the Flying Childers Stakes at Doncaster on September 12, 2014, ridden by George Baker. He looked to have the race won when, close to the line, the horse veered right and deposited Baker on the deck. Who was the horse?

6. Jellaby was second in the 1977 Lockinge Stakes at Newbury but in 1978, under Brian Taylor, he looked to have put that right when going clear well inside the final furlong. It was at this point that the unfortunate animal put his foot in the only hole on the course, stumbled and unseated Taylor. Given the eventual winner's name, perhaps the Mafia had something to do with it! What was it called?

7. The most well-known hard luck story concerns the 1956 Grand National, where the Queen Mother's Devon Loch, with the race at its mercy, unaccountably collapsed on its belly a few yards from the line, bringing the phrase 'to do a Devon Loch' to the language. Who trained Devon Loch?

8. The 1988 edition of the King George V Handicap at Royal Ascot saw Ile De Chypre, trained by Guy Harwood and ridden by Greville Starkey go clear inside the final furlong before suddenly veering left towards the stands and unseating his jockey. What was the name of the horse, trained by Geoff Lewis and ridden by Tony Culhane, who won the race?

9. In October 2006, it looked like another winner for the Richard Johnson and Philip Hobbs combination when their charge went clear at Exeter. However, yards from the line the horse decided it had had enough and lay down on the track, catapulting Johnson past the post but with no desire to get there itself. What was it called?

10. On January 15, 2009, at Taunton, all Dave Nevison asked of the horse trained by Neil Mulholland and ridden by James Davies was that it amble past the winning post to win a race in which it was five lengths clear and secure him a sum north of £250,000. Near the line it suddenly jinked and the jockey hit the ground like a sack of spuds. The horse's name was the opposite of Dave's despair, which was bottomless. What was it called?

'VANISHED INTO THIN AIR!' – DEFUNCT RACECOURSES.

1. Racing took place on this Surrey course between 1890 and 1962. After surviving a suffragette-inspired arson attack it went on to host the Triumph Hurdle from 1939 until the course's closure. Mansfield Town FC bought one of its grandstands and Ascot acquired 20 acres of its turf for its new jumps track.

2. Despite its demise in 1977 this small Scottish venue, whose beginnings are lost in the mists of time, could claim to have inaugurated the world's oldest race, for which a silver bell was the winner's reward. After a gap of over 30 years, in 2008 the race found its way to Hamilton.

3. This venue's enduring claim to fame is that, on July 13, 1951, it staged England's first evening meeting. A well-known end-of-season handicap it used to hold is still run at Doncaster but this course's end came in 1964.

4. Nicknamed 'the frying pan' due to its unusual configuration, this atmospheric place in North London had its final meeting on Tuesday September 8, 1970, bringing down the curtain on 102 years of racing.

5. You might well ask! Racing began on this East Kent course in 1849. National Hunt racing eventually dominated proceedings on this small oval track until racing ended on May 2, 1974.

6. This course experienced both Flat and jumps racing between 1891 and 1940. It was initially in Surrey but border changes have now placed it in West Sussex. It hosted the First World War Grand Nationals of 1916, 1917 and 1918 but 'progress' eventually caught up with it and the area is now somewhat noisier than it once was!

7. This course, which sounds like Inspector Morse's sidekick, enjoyed over 200 years of racing on the slopes of the South Downs. After its closure on September 14, 1964, racing enthusiasts had to go west, to Brighton, for their sport, although the course is still used as a training centre.

8. This county capital saw racing from as early as 1727 when the Royal Plate was introduced, until the doors shut on racing for the last time in 1964, although its landmark handicap was immediately transferred to Doncaster where it still provides the curtain raiser to the Flat season.

9. The first recorded evidence of racing at Bromford Bridge was in 1895 and, like one of our earlier courses, the suffragettes had a real go at destroying it! It survived until June 21, 1965, when a Lester Piggott double gave the assembled company something to remember it by.

10. Located west of town in Westenhanger, when this course opened in 1898 a local paper envisaged the French braving the Channel crossing to support the venture but even the eventual advent of the Tunnel failed to produce the desired invasion and a variety of problems led to it being the last of our courses to disappear when it went under in 2012.

'WET STUFF.' RIVERS, SEAS, OCEANS AND THE LIKE.

1. An exhilarating front-running performance by this horse brought the 2018 Cheltenham Gold Cup to Richard Johnson and Colin Tizzard.

2. This filly, trained by William Haggas and ridden by James Doyle, took the 2018 edition of the Irish Oaks.

3. Winner of a wartime Derby in 1944, owned by Lord Rosebery, trained by Jack Jarvis and ridden by Billy Nevett, they were probably all feeling like they were on the crest of a wave after it prevailed!

4. Brian Taylor was on board and Ryan Price saddled this winner of Ascot's Coventry Stakes in 1978.

5. Under French jockey Yves Saint-Martin and trained in France by Angel Penna, this filly flew home in the 1976 1,000 Guineas at Newmarket.

6. The winner of the 1993 running of the Arc, trained by Jean Lesbordes and ridden by Eric Saint-Martin.

7. Oaks winner for jockey Johnny Murtagh and trainer William Haggas at Epsom in 2011.

8. Currently, this is Sir Michael Stoute's only winner of the Lincoln. It happened in 2005 and Robert Winston did the steering.

9. When this filly, trained by Richard Hannon jnr and ridden by Sean Levey, won the 2018 1,000 Guineas at Newmarket, the 66-1 you could have about her chances was the biggest in the nearly 240-year history of the race.

10. This horse, trained by Tom Jones, was a star turn in the 1970s at Sandown, where his jumping was so thrilling that there is a big race named in his honour at the Esher track each year.

WOMEN JOCKEYS – 20TH CENTURY.

1. Who created a new record for female jump jockeys with 22 wins in a season in 1979-80?

2. Who was the first woman to have a ride in the Grand National on Barony Fort in 1977?

3. Who rode Ten No Trumps to victory in the Dresden Diamond Stakes at Ascot for trainer Sir Michael Stoute in 1987?

4. The first woman to ride in the Derby on 500-1 shot Portuguese Lil in 1996 was also the first woman to ride a Group 1 winner the next year when Ya Malak dead-heated in the Nunthorpe Stakes. Who was she?

5. In American racing who made history in 1993 by being the first woman jockey to win a Triple Crown race when Colonial Affair won the Belmont Stakes?

6. Who, on Cheers in 1982, became the first woman to complete the Grand National course, finishing eighth?

7. Who, on her first ever ride, was the first female jockey to win a race in Britain when 50-1 shot Scorched Earth won at Kempton Park in May 1972?

8. Sprowston Boy's victory in the 1987 Queen Alexandra Stakes at Royal Ascot was the first time that a race at the meeting was won by a female jockey. Who was she?

9. The Sex Discrimination Act of 1975 meant that women could ride under National Hunt Rules and, in February 1976, Nicky Henderson's wife to be became the first to win such a race, at Stratford. Strangely enough, the second woman to ride a National Hunt winner was her twin sister, Jane, at Warwick. Who was she?

10. Which female jump jockey won twice at the Cheltenham Festival before competing unsuccessfully in the 1988 Grand National on a horse that had a shortened version of her own name?

WOMEN JOCKEYS – 21ST CENTURY.

1. The first professional female jockey from Scotland, at Musselburgh in February 2012, on Red Tanber for trainer Bruce Mactaggart, broke a 32-year-old record for the number of winners by a female jockey in a jumps season, with her 23rd win. Who was she?

2. Champion apprentice in 2016, in which year she recorded 87 wins, she opened 2017 with victory in Ascot's Victoria Cup aboard Fastnet Tempest for trainer William Haggas. Who was she?

3. The most successful female Flat jockey of recent times, in 2011 she won two Group 1 races, firstly in the July Cup on Dream Ahead and then on Margot Did in the Nunthorpe. Who was she?

4. Irish jump jockey from a well-known racing family who recorded the best performance from a female rider in the Grand National in 2012 when finishing third on Seabass. Who was she?

5. Who was the first woman jockey to win the Melbourne Cup, on Prince Of Penzance in 2015?

6. Trainer's daughter who took the 2012 apprentice title and, on Oaks day at Epsom, had a notable success aboard Laffan in the Investec Asset Management Handicap.

7. From a well-known racing dynasty, she became the first woman to ride a Grade 1 National Hunt winner when Noel Meade's Leading Run took the Champion Bumper at Punchestown in 2006.

8. She started out with John Oxx and was champion Irish female apprentice in 2004 before coming to England where she rode over 300 winners until a foot injury ended her career.

9. Rider associated with Kikonga, Saigon and Rewarded amongst others, her best season being in 2008 when she had 71 winners before an injury sustained at Brighton forced her retirement at the age of 29.

10. Tea For Two was to prove a good horse for this jump jockey because she became the first woman to ride a Grade 1 winner over obstacles on this horse in the Kauto Star Novices' Chase at Kempton in 2015 and followed up with the Betway Bowl at Aintree in 2017.

WOMEN TRAINERS – 20TH CENTURY.

1. She became the first woman to train a Grand National winner when Corbiere was successful in 1983.

2. If you consult the record books you will find that the trainer of Gilles De Retz, winner of the 1956 2,000 Guineas, was Charles Jerdein. Women could not offically be trainers in that era. Who really trained the horse?

3. Who, in August 1966, became the first woman to train a winner in Britain officially when she sent her horse Pat from her Binfield, Berkshire yard to Brighton where it prevailed on the day after her licence was granted? Incidentally, she carried on training until she was 90!

4. Which female trainer sent out Teeton Mill to win both the Hennessy Gold Cup and the King George VI Chase in 1998?

5. Her husband had already sent out a winner of two Champion Hurdles when she literally took over the reins in 1983, producing Gaye Brief to land the race again. Who was she?

6. Which French trainer won the British 1,000 Guineas three times between 1983 and 1992 and, for good measure, won it again in the next century?

7. When Shiny Copper won the 1982 running of the Triumph Hurdle at Cheltenham under jockey Allen Webb, which Pulborough-based trainer saddled the horse?

8. Which female trainer won three Chester Cups in the 1990s with Travelling Light and Top Cees?

9. Who was the first woman to train 100 winners in a calendar year, in 1991, and then, the following year, became the first female trainer to reach 50 winners on the Flat?

10. A major figure in the history of the struggle of female trainers, it was her successful challenge in the Court of Appeal in 1966 that enabled women to train under their own name for the first time. Earlier, in 1937, she had unofficially saddled Sandsprite to be second in the Derby.

WOMEN TRAINERS – 21ST CENTURY.

1. The Ebor has been a good race for female trainers. Who started the ball rolling in 2000 when, under a superb front-running ride by Pat Eddery, Give The Slip did just that to the rest of the field?

2. Who carried it on with 100-1 shock Mudawin in the same race in 2006 with John Egan aboard?

3. Who completed the treble in 2013 when Tom Queally steered Tiger Cliff to victory?

4. Who trained Jezki to win the Champion Hurdle in 2014 under Barry Geraghty?

5. Who had her first Group 1 and Royal Ascot winner when Accidental Agent won the 2018 renewal of the Queen Anne Stakes under jockey Charlie Bishop?

6. Who trained Sovereign Debt when he won the All-Weather Mile Championship at Lingfield in April 2017 under James Sullivan?

7. In 2013, Auroras Encore was a Grand National winner at 66-1 for jockey Ryan Mania and which trainer?

8. When Speciosa won the 2006 Oaks with jockey Michael Fenton it was the first time that a British woman had trained the winner of the race. Who was she?

9. Which trainer had a Royal Ascot winner in 2008 when the Sam Hitchcott-ridden Missoula took that year's Ascot Stakes?

10. Who was the only woman to train a winner at the 2019 Cheltenham Festival?

YOUR NUMBER'S UP!

All these winning horses contain a number in their name.

1. This horse, trained by Aidan O'Brien and ridden by Jamie Spencer, ruled Royal Ascot's King Edward VII Stakes in 2004.

2. Which horse, in 1954, became the only one to win the Cheltenham Gold Cup with two numbers in its name?

3. Which Pascal Bary-trained filly ran second to Russian Rhythm in the 1,000 Guineas of 2003 before landing the prestigious Breeders' Cup Mile at Santa Anita?

4. The 1966 Eclipse Stakes victor for Vincent O'Brien and Lester Piggott sounds like a piece of dialogue from Robert Stevenson's 'Treasure Island.'

5. Having just backed this Richard Hughes/Roger Charlton colt for the 2003 Coventry Stakes at Ascot, there was a knock at the door and two men from a water company stood there with his name emblazoned on their jackets. Couldn't lose, could it?

6. Katie Walsh lit up Cheltenham with this Willie Mullins-trained winner of the 2010 County Hurdle who then went on to be placed in three successive Irish Champion Hurdles. Name the horse.

7. This Peter Nelson-trained horse, ridden by Jimmy Lindley, went like a rocket in the 1971 running of Goodwood's Stewards' Cup.

8. Extremely low energy reading for Greville Starkey and Guy Harwood's successful charge in the 1988 Ascot Stakes.

9. This American horse, winner of Grade 2 races in 2013 and 2014, was named ironically after a best-selling novel and eventually, in 2018, became the title of David Ashforth's book on racehorse names.

10. Ruby Walsh and Willie Mullins took the Ballymore Properties Novices' Hurdle at the 2008 Cheltenham Festival with a horse who sounds like it's got three numbers in its name but turns out to just have two.

ANSWERS

QUIZ No 1. ACTORS, FILMS AND RELATED STUFF.

1. Astaire.

2. Invisible Man.

3. Crocket.

4. Notnowcato.

5. Brando.

6. Gielgud.

7. Redford.

8. Humphrey Bogart.

9. The Bunny Boiler.

10. Oscar Schindler.

QUIZ No 2. ADVERTISING.

1. Seagram.

2. Canon Can.

3. Go Shell.

4. Ovaltine.

5. England's Glory.

6. The Grand National.

7. Friar's Balsam.

8. Night Nurse.

9. Schweppshire Lad.

10. Oxo.

Answers

....

QUIZ No 3. AFTER YOU, SIR!

1. Sir Percy.

2. Sir Michael.

3. Sir Montagu.

4. Sir Harry Lewis.

5. Sir Rembrandt.

6. Sir Ivor.

7. Sir Gerry.

8. Sir Peter Teazle.

9. Sir Gallahad III.

10. Sir Francis.

QUIZ No 4. 'ANIMAL HOUSE.'

1. Little Wolf.

2. Roaring Lion.

3. Papal Bull.

4. Tiger Roll.

5. Oriental Fox.

6. Peeping Fawn.

7. Brown Panther.

8. The Lamb.

9. Turtle Island.

10. The Leopard.

QUIZ No 5. THE ARC.

1. Star Appeal.

2. Because the winner was trained by Alec Head and ridden by Freddy Head.

3. Peintre Celebre and Olivier Peslier.

4. Zarkava (2008).

5. Frankie Dettori (six).

6. Sagace.

7. Dalakhani.

8. Chantilly.

9. Treve (2013).

10. Yves Saint-Martin (four) and Eric Saint-Martin (one).

QUIZ No 6. 'ASCOT ATTACK' – PART ONE.

1. Cash Asmussen.

2. Gary Stevens.

3. Brent Thomson.

4. Steven Arnold.

5. John Velasquez.

6. Joel Rosario.

7. Zac Purton.

8. Luke Nolen.

9. Craig Newitt.

10. Jay Ford.

Answers

QUIZ No 7. 'ASCOT ATTACK' – PART TWO.

1. Mikel Delzangles.

2. Wesley Ward.

3. Daniel Morton.

4. Danny Shum.

5. Ugo Penco.

6. Peter Moody.

7. John Hammond.

8. Lee Freedman.

9. Paul Perry.

10. Joe Janiak.

QUIZ No 8. ASSORTED COLOURS.

1. Black Ice.

2. Big Orange.

3. Silver Patriarch.

4. Brown Lad.

5. First Gold.

6. Yellow God.

7. Grey Swallow.

8. Green Desert.

9. Pink Gem.

10. Amber Rama.

QUIZ No 9. AUSTRALIAN JOCKEYS.

1. Rae Johnstone.

2. Jack Purtell.

3. Pat Glennon.

4. Ron Hutchinson.

5. Russ Maddock.

6. Bill Pyers.

7. Neville Sellwood.

8. Garnet Bougoure.

9. Scobie Breasley.

10. Bill Williamson.

QUIZ No 10. BIRDS.

1. Cormorant Wood.

2. My Swallow.

3. Little Owl.

4. Sea Pigeon.

5. Erimo Hawk.

6. Flakey Dove.

7. Wings Of Eagles.

8. Sea-Bird.

9. Crow.

10. Hawk Wing.

Answers

QUIZ No 11. 'THE BLUES.'

1. Blue Dakota.

2. Blue Wind.

3. Blue Cashmere.

4. Blue Peter.

5. Blue Monday.

6. Blue Duster.

7. Blue Point.

8. Blue Bunting.

9. Blue Bajan.

10. Blue Lamp.

QUIZ No 12. BOOKMAKERS.

1. Sunderlands.

2. Bet With Coral.

3. Barry Dennis.

4. Ladbrokes.

5. Victor Chandler.

6. John Banks.

7. William Hill.

8. bet365.

9. Gary Wiltshire.

10. Freddie Williams.

QUIZ No 13. THE CHELTENHAM FESTIVAL.

1. Golden Miller, Arkle, Dawn Run and Best Mate.

2. Dorothy Paget (1930s, 1940s, 1950s).

3. Viking Flagship.

4. Espoir D'Allen and Mark Walsh.

5. Harbour Pilot.

6. Marlborough.

7. Al Boum Photo.

8. Willie Wumpkins.

9. The Dikler.

10. Coneygree.

QUIZ No 14. CITIES.

1. Troy.

2. Dallas.

3. Paris.

4. Detroit.

5. Johannesburg.

6. Toulon.

7. Seattle Slew.

8. Rome.

9. Bangalore.

10. Zagreb.

Answers

QUIZ No 15. CLASSICAL COMPOSERS.

1. Mahler.

2. Beethoven.

3. Stravinsky.

4. Salieri.

5. Ravel.

6. Mozart.

7. Brahms.

8. Bach.

9. Monteverdi.

10. Debussy.

QUIZ No 16. CRYPTIC HORSES.

1. Run For Free.

2. Reel Buddy.

3. Var.

4. Punch.

5. Norton.

6. Wise Dennis.

7. Mine.

8. She was Veiled.

9. Kissing Cousin.

10. Just A Par.

QUIZ No 17. CRYPTIC 1,000 GUINEAS.

1. Fleet.

2. Waterloo.

3. Nocturnal Spree.

4. One In A Million.

5. On The House.

6. Pebbles.

7. Musical Bliss.

8. Cape Verdi.

9. Miss France.

10. Winter.

QUIZ No 18. CRYPTIC 2,000 GUINEAS.

1. Lomond.

2. Pall Mall.

3. Brigadier Gerard.

4. Mon Fils.

5. Wollow.

6. George Washington.

7. Cockney Rebel.

8. Night Of Thunder.

9. Gleneagles.

10. Churchill.

Answers

QUIZ No 19. CRYPTIC DERBY.

1. Never Say Die.

2. Santa Claus.

3. Nijinsky.

4. Slip Anchor.

5. Dr Devious.

6. Commander In Chief.

7. High Rise.

8. Oath.

9. Galileo.

10. High Chaparral.

QUIZ No 20. CRYPTIC OAKS.

1. Homeward Bound.

2. Sleeping Partner.

3. Dunfermline.

4. Balanchine.

5. Reams Of Verse.

6. Casual Look.

7. Ouija Board.

8. Light Shift.

9. Talent.

10. Minding.

QUIZ No 21. CRYPTIC ST LEGER.

1. Premonition.

2. Indiana.

3. Kew Gardens.

4. Touching Wood.

5. Airborne.

6. Intermezzo.

7. Sixties Icon.

8. Masked Marvel.

9. Simple Verse.

10. Capri.

QUIZ No 22. CRYPTIC GRAND NATIONAL.

1. Well To Do.

2. Rag Trade.

3. Ben Nevis.

4. Hallo Dandy.

5. Papillon.

6. Silver Birch.

7. Comply Or Die.

8. Don't Push It.

9. Many Clouds.

10. Rule The World.

Answers

QUIZ No 23. CRYPTIC CHAMPION HURDLE.

1. Winning Fair.

2. Comedy Of Errors.

3. Make A Stand.

4. Monksfield.

5. For Auction.

6. Granville Again.

7. Collier Bay.

8. Rooster Booster.

9. Katchit.

10. Hurricane Fly.

QUIZ No 24. CRYPTIC CHELTENHAM GOLD CUP.

1. Patron Saint.

2. Red Rower.

3. Knock Hard.

4. Ten Up.

5. Dawn Run.

6. The Thinker.

7. See More Business.

8. War Of Attrition.

9. Bobs Worth.

10. Lord Windermere.

QUIZ No 25. CRYPTIC QUEEN MOTHER CHAMPION CHASE.

1. Dunkirk.

2. Flyingbolt.

3. Muir.

4. Crisp.

5. Another Dolly.

6. Buck House.

7. Katabatic.

8. Moscow Flyer.

9. Dodging Bullets.

10. Special Tiara.

QUIZ No 26. CRYPTIC KING GEORGE VI CHASE.

1. Halloween.

2. Mandarin.

3. Dormant.

4. Titus Oates.

5. Barton Bank.

6. One Man.

7. Silver Buck.

8. Kicking King.

9. Long Run.

10. Cue Card.

Answers

QUIZ No 27. CURRENT JOCKEYS – FLAT.

1. William Buick.

2. Oisin Murphy.

3. James Doyle.

4. Graham Lee.

5. Daniel Tudhope.

6. Silvestre de Sousa.

7. Adam Kirby.

8. Luke Morris.

9. Pat Cosgrave.

10. Jason Watson.

QUIZ No 28. CURRENT JOCKEYS – JUMPS.

1. Aidan Coleman.

2. Leighton Aspell.

3. Gary Moore and Jamie Moore.

4. Bryan Cooper.

5. Davy Russell.

6. Robbie Power.

7. Paddy Brennan.

8. Sean Bowen.

9. Harry Skelton.

10. Wayne Hutchinson.

QUIZ No 29. CURRENT TRAINERS – FLAT.

1. Snr.

2. Hughie Morrison.

3. Brian Ellison.

4. Charlie Appleby.

5. Roger Varian.

6. Mark Johnston.

7. Richard Fahey.

8. Kevin Ryan.

9. Ed Dunlop.

10. Michael Bell and William Haggas.

QUIZ No 30. CURRENT TRAINERS – JUMPS.

1. Jonjo O'Neill.

2. Dan Skelton.

3. Colin Tizzard (Cue Card and Thistlecrack).

4. Nigel Twiston-Davies.

5. Nick Williams.

6. Philip Hobbs.

7. Tom George.

8. Kim Bailey.

9. Warren Greatrex.

10. Harry Fry.

Answers

QUIZ No 31. 'DISTAFF.'

1. Mrs McArdy.

2. Sun Princess.

3. Godiva.

4. Mrs Penny.

5. Lady Carla.

6. Madam Gay.

7. Midway Lady.

8. Confidential Lady.

9. Jet Ski Lady.

10. Lady In Silver.

QUIZ No 32. 'FLAT HUNTING.'

1. Nicky Henderson.

2. Gordon Elliott.

3. Donald McCain.

4. Detroit City.

5. Eddie Ahern and Dale Gibson.

6. Domination.

7. Alan King.

8. Martin Pipe.

9. Andrea Atzeni.

10. David Pipe.

QUIZ No 33. FLOWERS AND PLANTS.

1. Larkspur.

2. Dahlia.

3. Rhododendron.

4. Juniper Girl.

5. Roses In May.

6. Desert Orchid.

7. Primula Boy.

8. Iris's Gift.

9. Hydrangea.

10. Floribunda.

QUIZ No 34. FOOTBALL.

1. Hunt Ball (Roger Hunt and Alan Ball).

2. Aston Villa.

3. Charlton.

4. Selhurstpark Flyer.

5. Chelsea.

6. Come On The Blues.

7. Chesterfield.

8. Ayala.

9. Charlie George.

10. Zidane.

Answers

QUIZ No 35. FRENCH JOCKEYS.

1. Christophe Lemaire.

2. Yves Saint-Martin.

3. Mickael Barzalona.

4. Roger Poincelet.

5. Olivier Peslier.

6. Gerald Mosse.

7. Thierry Jarnet.

8. Alain Lequeux.

9. Freddy Head.

10. Maxime Guyon.

QUIZ No 36. 'HISTORICAL FIGURES'.

1. Gladstone.

2. James Garfield.

3. Horatio Nelson.

4. Wainwright.

5. General Gordon.

6. Dick Turpin.

7. Caxton.

8. Parnell.

9. Thomas Chippendale.

10. Pheidippides.

....

QUIZ No 37. THE KING GEORGE VI AND QUEEN ELIZABETH STAKES.

1. Sir Michael Stoute (six up to 2018).

2. Mill Reef.

3. Galileo.

4. Lester Piggott (seven).

5. Germany (by Peter Schiergen).

6. Mick Kinane.

7. 'Postponed' won the race.

8. Dylan Thomas and Enable.

9. Noel Murless and Saeed Bin Suroor.

10. Nashwan.

QUIZ No 38. LINKS.

1. They are all found on the London Underground (Stratford, Warwick Avenue, Newbury Park and Leicester Square).

2. They have all written novels about horseracing.

3. They have all won the 2,000 Guineas.

4. They were the jockeys involved when Michael Dickinson famously trained the first five home in the 1983 Cheltenham Gold Cup.

5. They were all sired by Mill Reef.

6. They were the venues for AP McCoy's 1,000th, 2,000th, 3,000th and 4,000th winners respectively.

7. They were trained by three different O'Briens; Vincent, David and Aidan.

8. They are the only three horses of three letters to win the Oaks.

9. The Oaks.

10. Up to 2018, they are the only horses to have won the 'Whitbread' more than once.

Answers

QUIZ No 39. LITERATURE – PART ONE. BOOKS.

1. Julius Caesar.

2. Cider With Rosie.

3. Metroland.

4. The Go-Between.

5. The Great Gatsby.

6. Tale Of Two Cities.

7. Canterbury.

8. D'Urberville.

9. Ulysses.

10. Nicholas Nickleby.

QUIZ No 40. LITERATURE – PART TWO. WRITERS.

1. Dylan Thomas.

2. Dickens Hill.

3. Yeats.

4. Pasternak.

5. Oscar Wilde.

6. The Bard.

7. Simenon.

8. Byron.

9. Boswell.

10. Orwell.

QUIZ No 41. 'LOCATION, LOCATION, LOCATION' – PART ONE. THE FLAT.

1. Haydock.

2. Doncaster.

3. Newmarket.

4. Windsor.

5. Ripon.

6. York.

7. Epsom.

8. Redcar.

9. Goodwood.

10. Chester.

QUIZ No 42. 'LOCATION, LOCATION, LOCATION' – PART TWO. JUMPS.

1. Chepstow.

2. Newbury.

3. Newcastle.

4. Ascot.

5. Huntingdon.

6. Fairyhouse.

7. Sandown.

8. Wincanton.

9. Cheltenham.

10. Wetherby.

Answers

QUIZ No 43. LOOSE LETTERS.

1. Andrasch Starke and Greville Starkey.

2. P. Beasley and A. Breasley (Scobie).

3. Arrogate and Harrogate.

4. Rule The World (Grand National) and Ruler Of The World (Derby).

5. Unite.

6. Pentire.

7. A.C. Milan and Milan.

8. Joe Orton and John Gorton.

9. Punchestowns and Punchestown.

10. Scorpio and Scorpion.

QUIZ No 44. 'M's IN THE LEGER.

1. Moon Madness.

2. Minster Son.

3. Michelozzo.

4. Moonax.

5. Mutafaweq.

6. Millenary.

7. Milan.

8. Mastery.

9. Masked Marvel.

10. Meld.

QUIZ No 45. THE MISSING WORD ROUND – PART ONE. THE FLAT.

1. Jack.

2. Star.

3. Light.

4. Island.

5. Lady.

6. Society.

7. Look.

8. Swing.

9. Cover.

10. Sergeant.

QUIZ No 46. THE MISSING WORD ROUND – PART TWO. THE JUMPS.

1. Silver.

2. Call.

3. Cottage.

4. Flagship.

5. Dawn.

6. Party.

7. Mill.

8. Master.

9. Run.

10. Pigeon.

Answers

QUIZ No 47. THE MISSING WORD ROUND – PART THREE. JOCKEYS, TRAINERS AND OWNERS.

1. Nelson.

2. George.

3. Barry.

4. Ryan.

5. Dick.

6. Martin.

7. Cecil.

8. Keith.

9. Raymond.

10. Winston.

QUIZ No 48. 'MOONING' (Tastefully, of course).

1. Hunter's Moon.

2. Moonstone.

3. Lucky Moon.

4. Moon Ballad.

5. Spanish Moon.

6. Moon Storm.

7. Sea Moon.

8. Moon Mountain.

9. Pether's Moon.

10. Purple Moon.

QUIZ No 49. NATIONALITIES.

1. Scottish Rifle.

2. Swiss Maid.

3. Greek Dance.

4. Belgian Bill.

5. Spanish Steps.

6. Irish Ball.

7. Indian Skimmer.

8. Welsh Pageant.

9. Russian Rhythm.

10. Dutch Art.

QUIZ No 50. NO MEAN FEAT.

1. Sir Mark Prescott.

2. Aidan O'Brien.

3. Noel Murless.

4. Tom Dreaper.

5. David 'Dandy' Nicholls.

6. Dermot Weld.

7. Ryan Price.

8. Basil Briscoe.

9. Francois Doumen.

10. John Berry.

Answers

QUIZ No 51. OCCUPATIONS.

1. Chandler.

2. Taxidermist.

3. The Docker.

4. Centurion.

5. The Cobbler.

6. Policeman.

7. Apothecary.

8. The Drummer.

9. The Bo'sun.

10. Pearl Diver.

QUIZ No 52. ODD ONE OUT.

1. Red Splash. The others won the Grand National whereas Red Splash won the initial running of the Cheltenham Gold Cup in 1924.

2. Walter Swinburn.

3. Ascot. The others are Classic venues.

4. Willie Carson. The others all had brothers who were jockeys whereas Carson had a son (I am aware that there are other possible answers to this question).

5. Snow Knight. The others all won the Oaks whereas he won the Derby.

6. Treasure Beach. Colm O'Donoghue rode Treasure Beach while the other three were all ridden by Seamie Heffernan.

7. Sir Henry Cecil.

8. Barry Hills. (He was second four times.)

9. John Gosden.

10. Sir Michael Stoute. (Kribensis in 1990).

QUIZ No 53. PAINTERS.

1. Caravaggio.

2. Giacometti.

3. Gustav Klimt.

4. Gainsborough.

5. Hans Holbein.

6. Bonnard.

7. Velasquez.

8. Botticelli.

9. Monet.

10. Pablo.

QUIZ No 54. POT LUCK.

1. Emlyn Hughes.

2. Luke Harvey.

3. Kevin Darley.

4. John Egan.

5. Laura Mongan.

6. Ace Of Hearts and King Of Hearts.

7. Eddie Ahern, Adam Beschizza, Frankie Dettori, Johnny Murtagh and Jamie Spencer.

8. Lavinia Taylor, Hilary Parrott and Rebecca Curtis.

9. Caspian Prince.

10. Ask Tom and Tom Tate.

Answers

QUIZ No 55. RACECOURSES – PART ONE.

1. Chester. (For Hull City v Arsenal).

2. Redcar.

3. Perth.

4. Sedgefield.

5. Pontefract.

6. Ayr.

7. Catterick.

8. Beverley.

9. Aintree.

10. Hamilton.

QUIZ No 56. RACECOURSES – PART TWO.

1. Kempton.

2. Bath.

3. Limerick.

4. Ascot. (Tosca).

5. Tipperary.

6. Fontwell.

7. Newmarket.

8. Taunton.

9. Navan.

10. Sandown.

QUIZ No 57. 'REDS.'

1. Red Sea.

2. Red Alert.

3. Red Candle.

4. Red Cross.

5. Red Wine.

6. Red Evie.

7. Red Robbo.

8. Red Lancer.

9. Red Clubs.

10. He was Red Rum.

QUIZ No 58. REGAL BEASTS.

1. Royal Academy.

2. Royal Athlete.

3. Royal Rebel.

4. Royal Gait.

5. Royal Palace.

6. Royal Smoke.

7. Royal Frolic.

8. Royal Anthem.

9. Royal Relief.

10. Royal Applause.

Answers

QUIZ No 59. ROCK/POP/JAZZ/BLUES.

1. Partners in Jazz.

2. Deacon Blues.

3. Band On The Run.

4. Radiohead.

5. Paul Jones.

6. Jukebox.

7. Duke Ellington.

8. West Side Story.

9. Roll-A-Joint.

10. Arnold Layne.

QUIZ No 60. ROYAL ASCOT.

1. York.

2. Steve Cauthen.

3. Geordieland.

4. Brown Jack.

5. Henry Cecil.

6. The Royal Hunt Cup.

7. They all won two different races at the same meeting.

8. Sole Power.

9. Lester Piggott.

10. Rheingold. (The jockeys were Yves Saint-Martin and Lester Piggott).

QUIZ No 61. 'SAINTS ALIVE.'

1. St Vincent.

2. St Nicholas Abbey.

3. St Francis.

4. Saint Alebe.

5. St Lucia.

6. St Paddy.

7. Saint Estephe.

8. St Helena.

9. Order Of St George.

10. St Simon.

QUIZ No 62. SPORT.

1. Bannister.

2. Murrayfield.

3. Leg Spinner.

4. Dart Board.

5. Butler's Cabin.

6. Daytona.

7. Jack Hobbs.

8. Sandwich.

9. Crystal Palace.

10. Brasher.

Answers

QUIZ No 63. 'THE SPORT OF KINGS'...

1. King's Best.

2. King's Signet.

3. Kingmambo.

4. Kings Lake.

5. Kingman.

6. King Midas.

7. King Of Kings.

8. Kingsgate Native.

9. Belmont King.

10. King's Road.

QUIZ No 64. ...'AND QUEENS.'

1. Queen's Pride.

2. Queen's Hussar.

3. Arabian Queen.

4. Queen's Taste.

5. Queen's Logic.

6. Homecoming Queen.

7. Queen's Birthday.

8. Queensberry.

9. Queen Of The Fairies.

10. Queen Of Sheba.

QUIZ No 65. 'STRANGELY ENOUGH' – PART ONE.

1. Hennessy. (It won the Whitbread, as was).

2. London and Bristol. (The horses were Waterloo and Temple Meads).

3. Seaman (1882) and Kirkland (1905).

4. George Baker.

5. Omerta.

6. Stan Moore. (Stanmore).

7. Sea Pigeon, Flakey Dove, Rooster Booster, Hurricane Fly and Charlie Swan.

8. Basil Fawlty.

9. The horse was called Floyd. (Jimmy Floyd Hasselbaink, Pink Floyd, Pretty Boy Floyd, Floyd Patterson, Ray Floyd and Floyd Road).

10. Richard Hughes. (Harmonic Way 1999. Tayseer 2000).

QUIZ No 66. 'STRANGELY ENOUGH' – PART TWO.

1. 101. (Duffield 53 and Eddery 48).

2. The National Hunt Form Book.

3. The Fellow.

4. Fred Winter (3) and Fred Rimell (2).

5. Motivator (2005).

6. Silence In Court.

7. Two of Aidan O'Brien's sons, Joseph and Donnacha, combined as a trainer and jockey of the winner to beat their father's horse, who finished second.

8. Mark Dwyer and Conor O'Dwyer.

9. Free Sweater.

10. Ruby Walsh and Sam Waley-Cohen.

Answers

QUIZ No 67. 'THREES' – PART ONE. HORSES.

1. Cottage Rake.

2. Persian War.

3. Sharpo.

4. Istabraq.

5. Arkle.

6. Best Mate.

7. Reve De Sivola.

8. Hatton's Grace.

9. See You Then.

10. Badsworth Boy.

QUIZ No 68. 'THREES' – PART TWO. JOCKEYS.

1. Pat Eddery.

2. Lester Piggott.

3. Geoff Lewis.

4. Steve Donoghue.

5. Doug Smith.

6. Gordon Richards.

7. Ron Hutchinson.

8. Jimmy Lindley.

9. Manny Mercer.

10. Fred Rickaby.

QUIZ No 69. 'THREES' – PART THREE. TRAINERS.

1. Lord Huntingdon (William Hastings-Bass).

2. Charles Elsey.

3. Francois Boutin.

4. Willie Stephenson.

5. Derrick Candy.

6. Jim Dreaper.

7. Paddy Prendergast.

8. Noel Murless.

9. Cecil Boyd-Rochfort.

10. Vincent O'Brien.

QUIZ No 70. TOP JOCKEYS – FLAT. FRANKIE DETTORI.

1. Mark Of Esteem (1996 2,000 Guineas).

2. York (2006 St Leger).

3. Electrocutionist.

4. Balanchine.

5. Prix du Jockey Club (French Derby).

6. Ian Balding.

7. Fujiyama Crest.

8. Galileo Gold (2,000 Guineas).

9. The Derby (He finally won it in 2007 on Authorized).

10. Prix de Diane (French Oaks).

QUIZ No 71. TOP JOCKEYS – FLAT.
KIEREN FALLON.

1. St Leger.

2. Ascot.

3. Tuning.

4. Cover Up.

5. Aaim To Prosper.

6. Islington.

7. Mr Dinos.

8. Society Rock.

9. Ed Dunlop (Ouija Board – Oaks) and Richard Hannon jnr (Night Of Thunder – 2,000 Guineas).

10. High Premium.

QUIZ No 72. TOP JOCKEYS – FLAT.
RYAN MOORE.

1. David Wachman (Legatissimo – 1,000 Guineas).

2. Workforce.

3. Adelaide.

4. Saxon Warrior.

5. Kevin Ryan.

6. Martin Pipe.

7. Mendelssohn.

8. 13-8.

9. Snow Fairy.

10. Carlton House.

QUIZ No 73. TOP JOCKEYS – FLAT.
LESTER PIGGOTT.

1. These were the four horses he finished second on in the Derby.

2. Northern Dancer.

3. Alleged.

4. Rodrigo De Triano (1992) and Shadeed (1985).

5. Peter Walwyn (Humble Duty, 1970 1,000 Guineas), Dermot Weld (Blue Wind, 1981 Oaks), Geoff Wragg (Teenoso, 1983 Derby).

6. Piggott partially severed his ear, requiring 31 stitches, in a starting stalls incident at Epsom that forced him to wear a special helmet in the Guineas.

7. His father, Keith Piggott.

8. Haydock.

9. Carnoustie.

10. 'Miss me?'

QUIZ No 74. TOP JOCKEYS – FLAT.
SIR GORDON RICHARDS.

1. A staggering 26.

2. Tuberculosis.

3. Lincoln.

4. Sunderland.

5. The Coventry Stakes.

6. Chepstow.

7. Sun Chariot.

8. Tudor Minstrel.

9. Sir Victor Sassoon.

10. Reform.

Answers

QUIZ No 75. TOP JOCKEYS – JUMPS.
JOHN FRANCOME.

1. Burrough Hill Lad.

2. Neville Crump.

3. Peter Scudamore.

4. News King.

5. Lanzarote.

6. Brown Chamberlin.

7. Al Kuwait.

8. Sea Pigeon.

9. Wayward Lad.

10. Midnight Court.

QUIZ No 76. TOP JOCKEYS – JUMPS.
RICHARD JOHNSON.

1. Menorah.

2. Flagship Uberalles.

3. Wishfull Thinking.

4. Lacdoudal and Monkerhostin.

5. Fighting Chance.

6. Rooster Booster.

7. Noel Chance.

8. Hereford.

9. Ludlow.

10. Mighty Man.

QUIZ No 77. TOP JOCKEYS – JUMPS. SIR ANTHONY McCOY.

1. Bounce Back.

2. Wichita Lineman.

3. Edredon Bleu.

4. Brighton.

5. Family Business.

6. Brave Inca.

7. Clan Royal.

8. Jim Bolger.

9. Twenty.

10. Blowing Wind.

QUIZ No 78. TOP JOCKEYS – JUMPS. RUBY WALSH.

1. The Irish Champion Hurdle.

2. Exotic Dancer.

3. Ted Walsh.

4. War Of Attrition.

5. Numbersixvalverde.

6. Klassical Dream.

7. Nichols Canyon.

8. Tom Mullins and Asian Maze.

9. Strong Flow.

10. Silviniaco Conti.

Answers

QUIZ No 79. TOP TRAINERS – FLAT. SIR HENRY CECIL.

1. Scotland.

2. Cecil Boyd-Rochfort.

3. The 2,000 Guineas – three times.

4. Ripon.

5. Greville Starkey.

6. Old Vic.

7. The Nassau Stakes.

8. Shirley Heights.

9. Pat Eddery (Bosra Sham and Lady Carla in 1996).

10. Richard Quinn (Love Divine, 2,000 Oaks) and Tom Queally (Frankel, 2011 2,000 Guineas).

QUIZ No 80. TOP TRAINERS – FLAT. JOHN GOSDEN.

1. Noel Murless and Vincent O'Brien.

2. Bates Motel.

3. Richard Hills (on Lahan) and Paul Hanagan (on Taghrooda).

4. Royal Heroine.

5. Wings Of Desire.

6. Oasis Dream.

7. Dar Re Mi.

8. Stradivarius.

9. Raven's Pass.

10. The Fugue.

QUIZ No 81. TOP TRAINERS – FLAT.
AIDAN O'BRIEN.

1. It was the first time that a father and son had combined as trainer and jockey to win the Derby (Aidan and Joseph).

2. Alexandrova.

3. Jamie Spencer (Brian Boru) and Frankie Dettori (Scorpion).

4. He trained the winners of all five Irish Classics.

5. Imagine and Yesterday.

6. Virginia Waters (1,000) and Footstepsinthesand (2,000).

7. Colm O'Donoghue (Qualify).

8. Leading Light.

9. 28.

10. Rock Of Gibraltar.

QUIZ No 82. TOP TRAINERS – FLAT.
VINCENT O'BRIEN.

1. More (he won nine).

2. Sadler's Wells.

3. Paul Cook.

4. The 1970s, three wins – Nijinsky, Roberto and The Minstrel.

5. Pat Eddery (1983 and 1984 2,000 Guineas).

6. The Ascot Gold Cup.

7. Caerleon.

8. Liam Ward.

9. Abergwaun.

10. Ireland's National Stakes (since 2009 named the Vincent O'Brien National Stakes).

Answers

QUIZ No 83. TOP TRAINERS – FLAT.
SIR MICHAEL STOUTE.

1. Five (1985 to 1989).

2. Zilzal.

3. Singspiel.

4. Marwell.

5. The Lockinge Stakes (Newbury).

6. Neither (they each have five).

7. The King George VI and Queen Elizabeth Stakes.

8. Ajdal.

9. Conduit.

10. Fair Salinia.

QUIZ No 84. TOP TRAINERS – FLAT.
SAEED BIN SUROOR.

1. Kerrin McEvoy (Rule Of Law, 2004 St Leger).

2. Sakhee.

3. Classic Cliche.

4. Kazzia.

5. Dubawi.

6. Swain.

7. Daylami.

8. Dubai Millennium.

9. Intikhab.

10. Fantastic Light.

QUIZ No 85. TOP TRAINERS – JUMPS.
NICKY HENDERSON.

1. Greenhope.

2. Fred Winter.

3. Zaynar.

4. Might Bite.

5. Peter Easterby.

6. Bellvano.

7. Jamie Osborne.

8. Barry Geraghty and Nico de Boinville.

9. Peace And Co and Top Notch (Hargam was third).

10. Zongalero.

QUIZ No 86. TOP TRAINERS – JUMPS.
THE McCAINS.

1. Noel Le Mare.

2. L'Escargot.

3. 12 stone.

4. Brian Fletcher, Tommy Stack and Graham Lee.

5. 12.

6. Peddler's Cross.

7. Jason Maguire.

8. The Fighting Fifth Hurdle.

9. Cinders And Ashes.

10. Weird Al.

Answers

QUIZ No 87. TOP TRAINERS – JUMPS. WILLIE MULLINS.

1. Hedgehunter.

2. Florida Pearl.

3. Un De Sceaux.

4. Gordon Elliott.

5. Quevega.

6. Glens Melody.

7. Champagne Fever.

8. Charlie Swan.

9. Arctic Fire.

10. Tourist Attraction.

QUIZ No 88. TOP TRAINERS – JUMPS. PAUL NICHOLLS.

1. Mick Fitzgerald (See More Business).

2. Master Minded.

3. Noel Fehily.

4. The King George VI Chase.

5. Celestial Halo (2008) and Zarkandar (2011).

6. Denman.

7. Neptune Collonges.

8. Big Buck's.

9. The Tingle Creek.

10. It was owned in partnership by his mother and father and named after the village in which Paul Nicholls grew up.

QUIZ No 89. TOP TRAINERS – JUMPS.
VINCENT O'BRIEN.

1. The Irish Grand National.

2. Tim Molony.

3. Mr A.S O'Brien (Vincent's brother, known as 'Phonsie').

4. No.

5. Yes (in 1955).

6. The King George VI Chase.

7. True (£7,665).

8. Willie Stephenson (Sir Ken), Nicky Henderson (See You Then), Colin Davies (Persian War) and Aidan O'Brien (Istabraq).

9. A converted RAF fighter plane. Needless to say, all three won!

10. Tudor Line.

QUIZ No 90. TOP TRAINERS – JUMPS.
THE PIPES.

1. The Martin Pipe Conditional Jockeys' Handicap Hurdle.

2. Baron Blakeney.

3. Freddie Starr.

4. Tony McCoy and Timmy Murphy.

5. Gaspara.

6. Well Chief.

7. David Johnson.

8. Liberman and Moon Racer.

9. Strands Of Gold and Celestial Gold.

10. Lough Derg.

Answers

QUIZ No 91. TRUE OR FALSE – THE FLAT.

1. False (Andrea Atzeni also did this on Kingston Hill and Simple Verse).

2. True.

3. True.

4. False (Gianfranco Dettori won on Bolkonski in 1975 and Wollow in 1976).

5. True (The horses were Ruler Of The World, Orchestra, Hans Holbein, US Army Ranger and Venice Beach).

6. False (John Dunlop did this in 1990 and 1991 with Salsabil and Shadayid).

7. False (He did this before on Sakhee in 2001 and Marienbard in 2002).

8. True (They've won 14).

9. False (Sinndar in 2000 and Galileo in 2001 both did it).

10. True.

QUIZ No 92. TRUE OR FALSE – THE JUMPS.

1. False (He was riding for Willie Mullins).

2. False (Barry Geraghty also has five).

3. True (John Francome, Robert Earnshaw and Graham Bradley).

4. False (Caughoo won at 100-1 in 1947).

5. True (Aubrey Brabazon, Pat Taaffe and Jim Culloty).

6. True (In 2014, 2016 and 2017).

7. True (Kicking King twice, followed by four for Kauto Star).

8. False (Rachael Blackmore had two winners; A Plus Tard and Minella Indo).

9. True.

10. False (In 1966 Arkle was returned the 1-10 winner).

QUIZ No 93. UNLUCKY LOSERS. 'BORN UNDER A BAD SIGN.'

1. Rock Roi.

2. Central House.

3. Dayjur.

4. The race was declared void because Alec Marsh, the Jockey Club's Senior Starter, sent them off early.

5. Cotai Glory.

6. Don.

7. Peter Cazalet.

8. Thethingaboutitis.

9. Out The Black.

10. Topless.

QUIZ No 94. 'VANISHED INTO THIN AIR' – DEFUNCT RACECOURSES.

1. Hurst Park.

2. Lanark.

3. Manchester.

4. Alexandra Park.

5. Wye.

6. Gatwick.

7. Lewes.

8. Lincoln.

9. Birmingham.

10. Folkestone.

Answers

QUIZ No 95. 'WET STUFF.'

1. Native River.

2. Sea Of Class.

3. Ocean Swell.

4. Lake City.

5. Flying Water.

6. Urban Sea.

7. Dancing Rain.

8. Stream Of Gold.

9. Billesdon Brook.

10. Tingle Creek.

QUIZ No 96. WOMEN JOCKEYS – 20TH CENTURY.

1. Lorna Vincent.

2. Charlotte Brew.

3. The Princess Royal.

4. Alex Greaves.

5. Julie Krone.

6. Geraldine Rees.

7. Meriel Tufnell.

8. Gay Kelleway.

9. Diana Thorne.

10. Gee Armytage (Gee-A).

QUIZ No 97. WOMEN JOCKEYS – 21ST CENTURY.

1. Lucy Alexander.

2. Josephine Gordon.

3. Hayley Turner.

4. Katie Walsh.

5. Michelle Payne.

6. Amy Ryan.

7. Nina Carberry.

8. Cathy Gannon.

9. Kirsty Milczarek.

10. Lizzie Kelly.

QUIZ No 98. WOMEN TRAINERS – 20TH CENTURY.

1. Jenny Pitman.

2. Helen Johnson Houghton.

3. Norah Wilmot.

4. Venetia Williams.

5. Mercy Rimell.

6. Criquette Head.

7. Dina Smith.

8. Lynda Ramsden.

9. Mary Reveley.

10. Florence Nagle.

Answers

QUIZ No 99. WOMEN TRAINERS – 21ST CENTURY.

1. Amanda Perrett.

2. Jane Chapple-Hyam.

3. Lady Cecil.

4. Jessica Harrington.

5. Eve Johnson Houghton.

6. Ruth Carr.

7. Sue Smith.

8. Pam Sly.

9. Suzy Smith.

10. Emma Lavelle.

QUIZ No 100. YOUR NUMBER'S UP!

1. Five Dynasties.

2. Four Ten.

3. Six Perfections.

4. Pieces Of Eight.

5. Three Valleys.

6. Thousand Stars.

7. Apollo Nine.

8. Zero Watt.

9. Fiftyshadesofhay.

10. Fiveforthree.